A CALL TO
GROWTH

A CALL TO
GROWTH

ESTABLISHING THE
GROWING BELIEVER

DR. BILLIE HANKS, JR.

INTERNATIONAL EVANGELISM ASSOCIATION
SALADO, TEXAS 76571

For more information about this ministry, write or call:

INTERNATIONAL EVANGELISM ASSOCIATION
PO BOX 1174
SALADO, TEXAS 76571 - 1174
(254) 947-3030

Or visit us on the World Wide Web at WWW.IEAOM.ORG

Printed in the United States of America

This book is
dedicated
to those who share
the vision of
Spiritual Multiplication.

CONTENTS

ACKNOWLEGEMENTS

"If you love Me. . . feed My lambs." (John 21:15)

A Call To Growth has involved five years of writing, field testing, and work on the part of many people who have prayerfully refined these intermediate level materials on Christ-centered spiritual relationships.

To the team of writers and other close friends who have lived this message and sought to share it with others, goes my deepest gratitude.

Without the editing and discipling skills of Dr. Bill Shell, the early coordination of Rev. Sam Cook, the literary and creative gifts of Rev. Dan Nelson and Mr. Walt Wooden, and the design and typesetting skills of Mr. Randy Ray, *A Call To Growth* would never have moved from concept to reality.

Randy Craig's enthusiastic lay leadership, Dr. Tim Beougher's textual research, Max Barnett's Biblical studies, Wayne Watts' inspirational writing, and the assistance of IEA's dedicated staff and interns have all been orchestrated by the Lord to produce *A Call To Growth*.

We are especially grateful for the pioneering pastors and churches who have helped refine this new process of assimilation during the years of field testing.

Collectively, we seek one common goal:
To see God's people personally *grow* and *multiply* as they share their faith in Christ!

"Go therefore and make disciples. . . teaching them to observe all that I have commanded you." (Matthew 28:19 & 20)

Billie Hanks, Jr.

11

WEEKLY
SPIRITUAL GROWTH
ASSIGNMENTS

". . . grow in the grace of and knowledge of our Lord Jesus Christ." (2 Peter 3:18, NIV)

GLOSSARY

TG   = *A Call To Growth* Timothy's Guide
LCD = *Lessons In Christian Discipleship* (located on page 141 of your Timothy's Guide)
SJ   = *Spiritual Journal*
QT   = Quiet Time

Be sure to space your spiritual growth assignments throughout each week.

In addition to these inspirational assignments, you will enjoy several *Spiritual Application Projects* which will be explained during your meetings.

"But in your hearts set apart Christ as Lord. Always be prepared to give an answer to everyone who asks you to give the reason for the hope that you have. But do this with gentleness and respect."
(1 Peter 3:15, NIV)

WEEKLY SPIRITUAL GROWTH ASSIGNMENT #1

1. Start enjoying daily QTs using your *Quiet Time Reading Guide* in Appendix A, page 231 of your Timothy's Guide. Be prepared to share your favorite personal insights next week.
2. Take sermon notes using your SJ. Be prepared to review highlights during your next meeting.
3. Memorize **ROMANS 3:23** along with its heading, *All Have Sinned*. It will be helpful if you both memorize using the same translation. Remember to quote the reference before and after each verse. Be prepared to share your verse next week.
4. Read the introduction and complete Lesson 1 in LCD located on page 145 of your Timothy's Guide.
5. Read TG, Chapter 1, *Adoration*. Mark meaningful highlights and come prepared to discuss them next week.

WEEKLY SPIRITUAL GROWTH ASSIGNMENT #2

1. Pray to be an empowered witness each day this week!
2. Continue your daily QTs using the *Quiet Time Reading Guide* (Appendix A). Be prepared to share your favorite personal insights next week.
3. Take sermon notes using your SJ. Be prepared to review highlights during your next meeting.
4. Memorize **ROMANS 6:23** along with its heading, *Sin Earns Spiritual Death*. Meditate on the meaning of this verse. Be prepared to share your verses next week.
5. Complete Lesson 2 in the LCD.
6. Read TG, Chapter 2, *Evangelism Flows Out of a Godly Life*. Mark meaningful highlights and come prepared to discuss them next week.

WEEKLY SPIRITUAL GROWTH ASSIGNMENT #3

1. Continue your daily QTs, praying to be an empowered witness! Be prepared to share your favorite personal insights next week.
2. Take sermon notes using your SJ. Be prepared to review high-

lights during your next meeting.

3. Memorize **HEBREWS 9:27** along with its heading, *All Die Physically*. Meditate on the meaning of this verse. Be prepared to share your verses next week.

4. Complete Lesson 3 in the LCD.

5. Read TG, Chapter 3, *Sharing a Word of Truth*. Mark meaningful highlights and come prepared to discuss them next week.

> During this coming week, you and your Discipler will enjoy completing a *Spiritual Application Project*.

WEEKLY SPIRITUAL GROWTH ASSIGNMENT #4

1. Share at least one word of truth with someone this week.

2. Continue your daily QTs, praying to be an empowered witness. Be prepared to share your favorite personal insights next week.

3. Take sermon notes using your SJ. Be prepared to review highlights during your next meeting.

4. Memorize **ROMANS 5:8** along with its heading, *Christ Died For Us While We Were Still Sinners*. Meditate on the deep meaning of this important verse. Be prepared to share your verses next week.

5. Complete Lesson 4 in the LCD.

6. Read TG, Chapter 4, *Intercession*. Mark meaningful highlights and come prepared to discuss them next week.

WEEKLY SPIRITUAL GROWTH ASSIGNMENT #5

1. Continue your daily QTs praying to be an empowered witness. Be prepared to share your favorite personal insights next week.

2. Take sermon notes using your SJ. Be prepared to review highlights during your next meeting.

3. Memorize **EPHESIANS 2:8 & 9** along with its heading, *By God's Love We Are Saved Through Faith*. Meditate on the meaning of these verses. Be prepared to share your verses next week.

4. Complete Lesson 5 in the LCD.

5. Read TG, Chapter 5, *Sharing Your Testimony*. Be sure to complete the *My Personal Testimony* section. Mark meaningful highlights and come prepared to share your personal testimony next week.

> During this coming week, you and your Discipler will enjoy completing a *Spiritual Application Project*.

WEEKLY SPIRITUAL GROWTH ASSIGNMENT #6

1. Practice sharing your personal testimony with two or more friends this week.
2. Continue your daily QTs, praying to be an empowered witness. Be prepared to share your favorite personal insights next week.
3. Take sermon notes using your SJ. Be prepared to review highlights during your next meeting.
4. Memorize **JOHN 1:12** along with its heading, *Believe and Receive*. Meditate on the meaning of this verse. Be prepared to share your verses next week.
5. Complete Lesson 6 in the LCD.
6. Read TG, Chapter 6, *Confession*. Mark meaningful highlights and come prepared to discuss them next week.

WEEKLY SPIRITUAL GROWTH ASSIGNMENT #7

1. Continue your daily QTs, praying to be an empowered witness! Be prepared to share your favorite personal insights next week.
2. Pray specifically for opportunities to start sharing a word of truth or your testimony with someone who needs Christ.
3. Take sermon notes using your SJ. Be prepared to review highlights during your next meeting.
4. Complete Lesson 7 in the LCD.
5. Read TG, Chapter 7, *Sharing God's Plan of Salvation*. Mark highlights as you read. Be prepared to start sharing the Bridge Illustration during the next session. Practice presenting one verse at a time with explanation before moving on to the next verse. To aid with retention, number the presentation steps in

your book.

6. Memorize *The Sinners Prayer* included in your Scripture memory cards. Be prepared to share it next week.

> During this coming week, you and your Discipler will enjoy completing a *Spiritual Application Project.*

WEEKLY SPIRITUAL GROWTH ASSIGNMENT #8

1. Practice presenting the Bridge Illustration with a Christian friend this week.
2. Continue your daily QTs, praying to be an empowered witness! Be prepared to share your favorite personal insights next week.
3. Take sermon notes using your SJ. Be prepared to review highlights during your next meeting.
4. Memorize **PSALM 119:11** and meditate on this verse. Be prepared to share your verses next week.
5. Complete Lesson 8 in the LCD.
6. Read TG, Chapter 8, *Petition.* Mark meaningful highlights and come prepared to discuss them next week.

WEEKLY SPIRITUAL GROWTH ASSIGNMENT #9

1. Share the Bridge Illustration with a non-Christian this week.
2. Continue your daily QTs, praying to be an empowered witness! Be prepared to share your favorite personal insights next week.
3. Take sermon notes using your SJ. Be prepared to review highlights during your next meeting.
4. Memorize **2 CORINTHIANS 5:17** and meditate on this verse. Be prepared to share your verses next week.
5. Complete Lesson 9 in the LCD.
6. Read TG Chapter 9, *Giving is Worship.* Mark meaningful highlights and come prepared to discuss them next week.

> During this coming week, you and your Discipler will enjoy completing a *Spiritual Application Project.*

WEEKLY SPIRITUAL GROWTH ASSIGNMENT #10

1. Continue your daily QTs, praying to be an empowered witness! Be prepared to share your favorite personal insights next week.
2. Take sermon notes using your SJ. Be prepared to review highlights during your next meeting.
3. Memorize **1 JOHN 5:13** and meditate on this verse. Be prepared to share your verses next week.
4. Read TG, Chapter 10, *Thanksgiving*. Mark meaningful highlights and come prepared to discuss them next week.
5. Pray for opportunities to share Christ this week.
6. Enjoy personal independent Bible Study by following the steps outlined in Appendix F. Be ready to share your favorite insights next week. Please note the importance of the genealogy, history, and Biblical background for this study.

WEEKLY SPIRITUAL GROWTH ASSIGNMENT #11

1. Continue daily Quiet Times and sermon note-taking using your SJ. When you finish the *Quiet Time Readings* in Appendix A, start in Matthew using the Bible reading schedule on page 88 of your SJ.
2. Memorize **JOHN 10:28** and meditate on this verse. You will want to have an expanded memory system so you can continue memorizing Scripture consistently. *Scripture Memory Packets* (52 weeks) and the *Victory Scripture Memory Booklet* series (26 weeks each book) are available. (See TG page 257 for these resources).
3. Study Appendix H and mark the approaches you feel most comfortable using in the future.

INSPIRATIONAL READING

Chapters
1 – 10

CHAPTER 1

ADORATION

When considering the person of God, the Psalmist declared: "How great is Thy goodness...!" (Psalm 31:19a) Many centuries later, the hymnwriter, Stuart K. Hines, perhaps contemplating this same truth, wrote some of the world's most beloved lyrics:

> O Lord my God! When I in awesome wonder
> Consider all the worlds* Thy hands have made,
> I see the stars, I hear the rolling* thunder,
> Thy power throughout the universe displayed,
> Then sings my soul, my Savior God to Thee:
> How great Thou art, How great Thou art!

Since earliest times, man has stood in awe of the majesty and wonder of God and His power, as revealed in creation. But it is in the Bible that we come to understand the personal nature of God's love and His involvement with those who believe in Him.

Moses witnessed God's powerful protection as plague after plague was sent against the mighty army of Egypt. With each miracle, the ancient world was drawn to a deeper respect for

---

*Author's original words are "works" and "mighty." Copyright 1953, renewed 1981 by Manna Music, Inc., Denmere Ave., Burbank, CA 91504. International copyright secured. All rights reserved. Used by permission.

Jehovah God. At last, the children of Israel who had long been in bondage, were set free. They were led by a pillar of fire by night and a special cloud during the day. The sea opened before them, allowing safe passage to freedom, and it closed behind them, destroying that era's mightiest army on earth. Their sandals withstood the torturous elements; food and water were supplied in abundance in the wilderness. In addition, God audibly spoke to Moses and showed him the glowing beauty and awesome power of His presence (Exodus 7-17; 24:15 ff.; Deuteronomy 21:5).

Moses understood more about God than any man who had ever lived prior to his day, yet even he was aware that he had only *begun* to understand God's greatness. In the last days of his life, at the ripe old age of 120, he prayed earnestly to the Lord, saying "O Lord God, Thou has *begun* to show Thy servant Thy greatness and Thy strong hand...who can do such works and mighty acts as Thine?" (Deuteronomy 3:24)

COMMUNICATING LOVE FOR GOD

Adoration is expressed in many ways because of our various personalities and gifts. Because we feel love, we want to communicate it. Ultimately, the language of the heart will find its highest expression in talking with God about Himself. This unique kind of prayer is called Adoration. Through it, we praise God for *who* He is. The more you learn about Him, the more you will understand how little you really know! The joy of that continuing discovery and loving mystery causes us to live in a sense of expectation. This is much deeper than simply praying a prayer.

Few Christians have a crisp, clear understanding of this subject. They tend to confuse adoration with thanksgiving. When we thank God for *what* He does, we are gratefully recognizing His answers to our *petitions*. Adoration, on the other hand, focuses on God Himself, rather than the things He does.

The Psalmist said, "O Lord, our Lord, How majestic is Thy name in all the earth." (Psalm 8:1a) But I would guess that only a small percentage of a thousand unrehearsed prayers will be expressions of adoration. How often do you hear a person pray, "Lord, You are faithful. Your love is everlasting. Your wisdom is perfect. What an honor it is to be Your child?"

You may be saying, "I don't feel comfortable telling God things like that." Do you remember your first date or the first time you tried to say, "I love you?" Though everything in you knew that to be true, still the words were hard to say. But when they finally came, they meant so much to the one you loved. Adoration is like that. God is waiting for a generation of people who will be shamelessly head-over-heels and openly in love with Him. Why? Is it because God's ego needs to be stroked? No! It's because He knows that we need to learn how to express our love. To say, "God, I love You. You are great!" will not embarrass Him, and it shouldn't embarrass you.

If we infrequently offer prayers of adoration, what kind of praying does receive the majority of our attention? Petition is probably our most frequent form of prayer. While all earnest prayer is pleasing to God, there will be no prayers of petition in heaven, just adoration. We may make requests of God during our time on earth, but throughout eternity, as Christians, we will continue to joyfully speak to God about His glory with words like these: "Thou art worthy, O Lord, to receive glory and honor and power: for Thou hast created all things..." (Revelation 4:11, KJV) This kind of prayer flows out of your closest moments of fellowship with God. It is the highest form of praise. It is speaking to God from the depths of your heart, letting Him know how much you love Him and how special He is to you.

God cannot be corrupted by our praise. The sin of pride is completely foreign to His character. If you are a parent, His response to our adoration can be easily understood. Our prayers mean as much to Him as sweet words of love mean to you when spoken by your child. He receives them as a blessing. The psalmist says, "I will bless the Lord at all times; His praise shall continually be in my mouth." (Psalm 34:1) Surely this must be one of the greatest theological mysteries in all the Bible. How is it that you and I can "bless" God? How can small, frail creatures like us be so honored as to bless the infinite Creator?

I've thought about this question many times and I still do not comprehend the answer, but in some wonderful way when we adore Him it pleases Him. Perhaps it is because our adoration is not pre-programmed but an act of free will. Whatever the reason may be, the Bible says that when we sincerely tell God that we love Him and enjoy Him, He appreciates it.

OUR UNIQUENESS

Man was created for the purpose of knowing and loving God. Because we alone are made in His image, we have the privilege of prayer. No other creation in nature has that ability...not the tallest tree, the greatest mountain, or the clearest glacier can speak His name. When you express adoration to God, you are living out the evidence that you are different from everything else in the universe that He has made.

Among the majestic stars of heaven, the galaxies and myriads of creations, we alone can love God. He made us with the full ability to adore, love, respect and honor Him. Yet, He gave us a will which is free to apply or neglect that sacred ability. Understanding that, will have a profound impact on your life. Why? Because those who miss the privilege of loving Him might as well have *never been*. Like a flower that never bloomed, they failed to accomplish their sole purpose in life.

How ironic it is that mankind offers so little adoration, when that is our crowning privilege as human beings. If a person never loves God, he forfeits his divinely given means to inner fulfillment. He is left with a restlessness and a void that no other quality of love can fill.

HOW TO OFFER ADORATION

If we really love God, we will find a way to express it. One Father's Day, when my older daughter, Heidi, was about 10, I called her long-distance and said, "Honey, it's Father's Day, and there is a certain present I would like. Would you be willing to memorize some verses for me as my gift for Father's Day this year?" She said, "Oh, no, Daddy. I can't do that. I have already promised that to the Father for Father's Day." I was stunned by her response. The focus of her attention was totally upon God. No one ever told her to give Him a Father's Day present. Her adoration was deeper than words; it was an all-encompassing attitude which found a natural channel of expression.

The words of David, the shepherd boy, appear to be written with effortless sincerity. Psalm 23 affirmed a fact which he knew to be true: the Lord was his shepherd just as surely as he was the shepherd of his own flock. Why do we love that psalm so much? Out of 150 psalms it is perhaps the best known around the world. His attention is not on the sheep, but on the shepherd. "*He* makes me lie down... *He* leads... *He* restores... *He* guides." When David reflects upon the source of his courage, he quickly says, "*Thou* art with me... It is *Thy* rod and *Thy* staff that comfort me." Throughout the passage, David is calling our attention to God's faithfulness. Though this psalm is not a prayer in the usual sense of the word, it is nevertheless an unforgettable expression of David's adoration.

We do not have to be able to write like David to achieve this dimension of praise. God gave us the Bible so that in our hearts we can identify with the words of each of its approximately forty inspired authors. In your Quiet Time, through the ministry of the Holy Spirit, you can feel and express the same kind of attitudes and emotions as those who penned the thoughts you are reading.

On a strictly human level, this concept can be seen on Father's and Mother's Days and on other special occasions when expressions of love are shared through cards written by gifted authors. The words find their meaning in the fact that we have chosen them, not in the fact that we have written them.

In all of history, the foremost example of how to offer adoration was given to us by God rather than man. It was He who taught us the value of praise. When Jesus had reached mature manhood at the age of thirty, it was the Father who publicly expressed adoration for His only Son. When the prophet John the Baptist baptized Jesus, a voice from heaven said, "This is My beloved Son, in whom I am well pleased." (Matthew 3:17) The Father expressed His adoration in the form of a testimony.

When the Lord taught His disciples to pray, He specifically began with words of adoration for the Father: "Our Father who art in heaven, hallowed be Thy name. Thy kingdom come. Thy will be done, on earth as it is in heaven." (Matthew 6:9 & 10) It is easy to recognize the majestic quality of praise for God as perfected in Jesus' prayer. That same spirit, that same high exaltation is also present in 1 Chronicles 29:10 & 11 in the prayer of David. "So, David blessed the Lord in the sight of all the assembly; and David said, 'Blessed art Thou, O Lord God of Israel our father, forever and ever. Thine, O Lord, is the greatness, and the power, and the glory, and the victory, and the majesty, indeed, everything that is in the heavens and the earth; Thine is the dominion, O Lord, and Thou dost exalt Thyself as head over all.'" (1 Chronicles 29:10 & 11) David *blessed* the Lord. Typically, in the Hebrew sense the word blessed meant to give a bountiful gift of praise. And David praised his God publicly, in the presence of all the congregation.

Prayers of adoration are not only for our quiet times alone with God; they are also appropriate when groups of Christians gather to worship the Lord. Whether alone or in front of all the people, David prayed with the intensity of one who truly desired to exalt God. The power, the glory, the majesty and the exalted adoration that David ascribed to God, were part of the reason for his affectionate and honored relationship with the Father.

GROWING IN ADORATION

One morning in my Quiet Time, I was reading one of David's prayers. I became caught up in the beauty and the majesty of it. The Lord so captivated my thoughts and my spirit through these few verses that I did not want to read any further. I simply wanted to stay there with Him, basking in the light and warmth of that newfound truth. On some mornings in your devotional life, you will not read a whole chapter; you may cover only a few verses, but they will be more than enough to bring you to the point of surrender, worship, and obedience. Don't force the moment. Stay there until God has finished the work He wants to do in your heart.

Quietly listening and allowing the Holy Spirit to help you visualize what the Scriptures describe will enhance and intensify the quality of your adoration.

Consider Paul's words to the early Christians who lived in the city of Colossae. In describing the Lord Jesus, he said, "And He is the image of the invisible God, the first-born of all creation. For by Him all things were created, both in the heavens and on earth, visible and invisible, whether thrones or dominions or rulers or authorities— all things have been created by Him and for Him. And He is before all things, and in Him all things hold together." (Colossians 1:15-17) These three powerful sentences rank among the most important in all the Scriptures. The one true God, who has been invisible to man, intentionally became visible once in human history. This is worthy of our total concentration.

As a president's wife or a queen holds the title of first lady of the land, Christ, in His humanity, holds the sacred title of the *first born* or most preeminent of all creation. Not only do we honor Him as God, but since He chose to become a man, we honor Him supremely in the human realm as well. Paul wrote that "everything, everywhere was created by Him and for Him." The entire universe and spiritual realms which man does not begin to understand are all His handiwork. Should it come as a surprise that awe and wonder frequently accompany our adoration when we come before the Living Christ in prayer? His name is above every name and the Scriptures declare that ultimately "at the name of Jesus every knee shall bow, of those who are in heaven, and on earth, and under the earth, and that every tongue shall confess that Jesus Christ is Lord, to the glory of God the Father." (Philippians 2:9-11)

As strange as it may seem, the vilest sinner, the cynical atheist, the most egotistical philosopher, and every other nonbeliever will join God's prophets and Christian saints offering prayers of adoration to the Lord Jesus Christ. Those who are saved will do this from the glory of heaven but the lost will do it from their chosen estrangement in hell. Adoration will be the universal experience of every human being who has ever lived. It will express the utter joy of the wise and the crushing disappointment of the fool.

LIMITLESS RICHES

Try to see what Paul is describing in this passage written to the

Christians in Rome: "Oh, the depth of the riches both of the wisdom and knowledge of God! How unsearchable are His judgments and unfathomable His ways! For who has known the mind of the Lord, or who became His counselor?" (Romans 11:33-34) How much would world leaders and educational institutions gladly give to obtain and understand the wisdom of God!

The truth Paul expressed many centuries ago is timeless. There is no end to the riches of God's wisdom and knowledge. All that contemporary society could give would not begin to compare with the value of these divine attributes. His decisions and choices are perfect and, though we may search and try our best to understand them, while on this side of heaven, some will remain mysteries to us. This is why God has said that "without faith it is impossible to please Him, for he who comes to God must believe that He is, and that He is a rewarder of those who seek Him." (Hebrews 11:6)

Seeking God and desiring to know Him more deeply should be the lifelong pursuit of every Christian. We look backward to the occasion when we were forgiven and cleansed. We look forward to Christ-likeness and the privilege of increased service and understanding. Throughout this journey, adoration is to be our constant companion.

"And though you have not seen Him, you love Him, and though you do not see Him now, but believe in Him, you greatly rejoice with joy inexpressible and full of glory." (1 Peter 1:8)

CHAPTER 2

EVANGELISM FLOWS OUT OF A GODLY LIFE

One of the most important lessons you will ever learn is that evangelism flows out of a godly life. You will win no more people and exert no more influence for the Savior than the quality of your life allows.

If you have had a genuine conversion experience and even know how to share it, but fail to develop a godly character that is conforming to the image of Christ, you will be barren and ineffective in personal evangelism. To say it plainly, you cannot expect to witness successfully while being content with a spiritually mediocre life.

THE CLEANSING POWER OF THE WORD OF GOD

What an encouragement it must have been for the early disciples when they heard Jesus say, "You are already clean because of the word I have spoken to you." (John 15:3, NIV) Just as a farmer prunes back his trees to produce a better yield, Jesus carefully groomed His apostles for effective service. Above all else, their lives had to be pure.

At the start of His own ministry, Jesus revealed the secret of how to live a pure and victorious life. He told the Tempter, "It is written: 'Man does not live on bread alone, but on every word that comes from the mouth of God.'" (Matthew 4:4, quoting from Deuteronomy 15:3, NIV) *It is daily intake and yieldedness to God's Word* that determines how He can use you. The Scriptures are our source of spiritual strength. They build a Christian character that meets the lifelong prerequisite for effective evangelism.

I seldom find a believer who does not desire to be used by God. But it is also true that I rarely meet a believer who understands the cost of being used by God.

Learning to live in *obedience* to God's will as revealed through His Word is the key to experiencing an abundant personal ministry. We know this because obedience was the preoccupation of Jesus during His earthly life. Paul wrote the church at Philippi: "Your attitude should be the same as that of Christ Jesus, Who ... made Himself nothing, taking the very nature of a servant, being made in human likeness. And being found in appearance as a man, He humbled Himself and became obedient to death—even death on a cross!" (Philippians 2:5-8, NIV)

To be fully effective in evangelism, we need to emulate Jesus in His great willingness to please the Father. *Obedience* to His leadership must become our continual and highest goal in life. This begins slowly and grows through wholehearted allegiance to God's Word.

A WINSOM WITNESS

Evangelism flows out of a well-balanced life. Your friendliness will allow people to identify with you in a natural way. People are attracted to those who know how to laugh, sing, engage in athletics and enjoy being *real*. This special quality of reality comes only from God, who is the source of our witness. Jesus spoke of that source, "The words I say to you are not just My own. Rather, it is the Father, living in Me, who is doing His work." (John 14:10, NIV)

The Father is the One who desires to do the work of witness through us. The key to making that witness natural is simply praying, "Lord, is this You prompting my concern? If it is, I am eager for You to speak. Please don't let me get in Your way. Just let me relax in faith as You do it through me."

God wills to work through us. Though in ourselves we cannot lead anyone to Christ, the Holy Spirit is faithful to do it. He uses us as instruments of witness out of the overflow of His new life within us. When we are yielded, evangelism is totally natural in the lives of believers because of the indwelling presence of the Spirit of God. "For it is God who is at work in you, both to will and to work for His good pleasure." (Philippians 2:13)

PURITY IN OUR CHARACTER IS A CHOICE

I have never known a man or a woman who has been significantly used by God, who has come to that place without gaining victory in the area of personal purity. Temptation is no respecter of persons, so everyone who works in the kingdom of God is going to be tempted in many ways during his life. Satan wants to destroy the testimony of Christians, so he tries to sully them and tempt them to compromise with sin. His objective is to produce the continual presence of guilt in our lives. However, Christ has given us His full and effective victory in this regard. The Scripture promises, "If we confess our sin, He is faithful and righteous to forgive us our sins and to cleanse us from all unrighteousness." (1 John 1:9)

Because temptations are going to come, you need to understand that your purity of thought and your singleness of purpose are of supreme importance to God. Your purity is not determined for you. It requires your personal choice. Ponder what the apostle Paul wrote to Timothy: "Now in a large house there are not only gold and silver vessels, but also vessels of wood and of earthenware, and some to honor and some to dishonor. Therefore, *if* a man *cleanses himself* from these things, he will be a vessel for honor, sanctified, useful to the Master, prepared for every good work." (2 Timothy 2:20 & 21, NIV)

In this passage, Paul explains to Timothy that there are four levels of ministry we can experience as believers. We can choose to be vessels of gold, silver, wood, or clay. Some of these articles are for higher purposes than others. You would not use a gold pot for cooking spaghetti. Your gold and silver vessels are your finest possessions. They are designed for beauty. Other articles in your home, however, are not as valuable and are designed for what Paul calls "dishonorable" purposes. These are made of wood and clay.

The key to a successful ministry is found in the phrase, "if a man cleanses himself. . ." In context, it speaks of abstaining from godless conversation (v. 16), wickedness (v. 19), lustful desires (v. 22), and foolish arguments (v. 23). All of these sins are choices having to do with our purity.

"If a man cleanses *himself*!" It does not say that we are to cleanse our spouse, children, friends and fellow believers. Nor does it say that others are to help cleanse us. It does say that I must cleanse *myself*.

If a man cleanses himself from these things, he will be an instrument for honorable purposes in the hands of God. The vessel that will honor God most will be the one that has chosen to be clean. He will be like gold or silver.

Tragically, many Christians settle for being pottery; they never bear an effective testimony, never really learn the Word of God or choose a life of uncompromising moral and ethical standards. Because of failure to aspire to be vessels of gold, they fail to lead others to Christ and make little impact on their family and friends.

The word "if" implies that each of us has this God-given choice. No one has been predestined to be impure; it is not foreordained that Christians be mediocre or half-hearted; it is not determined that we be undisciplined, unloving or unjoyful. In fact, the opposite is true. Jesus Christ came to give us life and to give it to us abundantly (see John 10:10). His plan for us is that we have a progressively upward journey with Him.

HUMILITY IS ALSO A PERSONAL CHOICE

I was visiting with Grady Wilson, my earliest Paul, on one occasion and asked him, "Grady, how do you and Billy Graham handle pride? How do you keep yourselves spiritually clean in that area?"

He answered, "We deal with it the way Peter instructed us. He said, 'Humble yourselves, therefore, under God's mighty hand.' (1 Peter 5:6, NIV) Humility is a personal daily choice. Don't ask God to humble you. Don't ask your wife to humble you. Don't ask your Christian friends to humble you. Humble yourself."

Grady continued, "Billie, the first time you ever pray for God to humble you, you will be in *big* trouble! God knows how to humble people. If you read the Old Testament, you will find several kings He humbled. You wouldn't want to go through what they did."

God once put a mighty ruler named Nebuchadnezzar out in the pasture lands to eat grass like a common animal because it took that to humble him (Daniel 4:31-36). In the end, the king said, I quit (Daniel 4:37). Ultimately, in the pursuit of a man's best interests, God can always humble him if he refuses to humble himself.

Paul later taught the same concept in his first letter to Timothy: "Train *yourself* to be godly." (1 Timothy 4:7, NIV) In his second letter he tells Timothy to cleanse *himself*. The theme is clear: Humble yourself. Train yourself. Cleanse yourself. Don't sit around and say, "God, when You finally make me humble and clean, then I will serve You."

It is far better for you to use your own volition to humble and cleanse yourself. Perhaps the highest privilege of being made in the image of God is your ability to choose your own character. You were forgiven at Calvary and now you have the God-given ability to decide to walk in purity on a daily, hourly basis.

PLAN AHEAD FOR VICTORY

To have a clean mind and a lifestyle of purity, you need to plan ahead to avoid temptation. You will have to discipline yourself carefully in what you read, in the entertainment in which you participate and in the choice of your companions.

"Leave the presence of a fool, or you will not discern words of knowledge." (Proverbs 14:7)

If you have trouble with an unclean mind, you cannot blame someone else for your condition. If you continue in sin, you are simply not facing your problem head on. "Finally, brethren, whatever is true, whatever is honorable, whatever is right, whatever is pure, whatever is lovely, whatever is of good repute, if there is any excellence and if anything worthy of praise, let your mind dwell on these things." (Philippians 4:8, NIV)

While preaching in Germany, I met a young man who had been spending all his time drinking and dancing in bars. The night he was saved, he asked me how to avoid sin in the future. He came from a handsome eastern race noted for their dark olive skin color. As we talked, he said, "Billie, I need some help because I have more spiritual problems than the average person. I have a theory. The darker a person's complexion, the more vulnerable he is to temptation."

I could not help but chuckle. His theory was not only humorous but unbiblical. The Scriptures state that all are tempted without distinction as to race, complexion, or nationality. Paul said very clearly, "No temptation has seized you except what is common to man. And God is faithful; He will not let you be tempted beyond what you can bear. But when you are tempted, He will also provide a way out so that you can stand up under it." (1 Corinthians 10:13, NIV)

I shared with my Christian friend a favorite illustration from the folklore of the American Indian.

A young brave came to a wise old chief and said, "Chief, I have small twin dogs. One of them is brown, the other speckled." He continued, "I am going to let these two small dogs fight. Can you tell me which one will win the fight?"

The old Indian smiled and answered, "The one you feed the most."

The chief's answer does not come from the Bible, but its practical application agrees with the Scriptures. As a Christian, you have two natures in conflict with one another. In daily experience it is a guaranteed result that the one you feed is the one that will win. You may be a dedicated, born-again believer and even called to a special form of ministry, but it is certain that the nature you feed— the old nature or the new nature—is the one that will become stronger and predominate.

In order to cleanse yourself daily, you will have to starve your old nature and feed your new nature with the Word of God, spiritual praise and fellowship with growing believers. The key is feeding on and obeying the Word of God daily through your quiet time and Bible study. This will develop gold and silver character qualities in your life.

There is only one kind of instrument that a skilled surgeon cannot use. He can use one that is bent, crooked, old, or new, but he cannot use a *dirty* instrument, no matter how perfect and beautiful it may be otherwise.

The same is true in the Christian life. The only kind of person God cannot and will not use is one who has a dirty life. He can use us in spite of our ignorance; He can use us with our personality defects and our idiosyncrasies. But He will never use a life characterized by impurity until it is cleansed.

If you desire to be used of God in multiplication evangelism, if you decide to be a godly man or woman, if you choose to be pure, if you plan to succeed in your ministry and if you trust Him to accomplish it through you, *then it is a foregone conclusion that you will have victory.* "The One who calls you is faithful and He will do it." (1 Thessalonians 5:24, NIV)

THE IMPORTANCE OF THE WORD OF GOD

It is impossible to conceive of a Christian having a strong evangelistic or training ministry without having a good grip on the Word of God. Every believer needs to develop a good working knowledge of the Bible.

This does not come easily or without opposition from Satan. He will do anything and everything to divert us from the Word of God. It takes great diligence to be in the Scriptures on a daily basis.

In order to have a productive evangelistic ministry, your daily walk needs to be consistent in the areas of quiet time, Bible study, and Scripture memory. "So then, just as you received Christ Jesus as Lord, continue to live in Him, rooted and built up in Him, strengthened in the faith as you were taught, and overflowing with thankfulness." (Colossians 2:6, NIV)

Paul complimented the church in Berea for their commitment to the Word of God; "Now the Bereans were of more noble character than the Thessalonians, for they received the message with great eagerness and examined the Scriptures *every day* ..." (Acts 17:11, NIV). Consistency builds usability. Your devotional life is the platform on which your ministry is built. The Scriptures will become an enriching and natural part of your life as you enjoy them daily.

RESPONSIBLE SPEECH

Jesus sternly warned His generation that they were accountable for their words. He said, "But I tell you that men will have to give account on the day of judgment of every careless word they have spoken. For by your words you will be acquitted and by your words you will be condemned." (Matthew 12:36, 37, NIV) Earlier He had said in the Sermon on the Mount, "Simply let your 'Yes' be 'Yes,' and your 'No,' 'No.'" (Matthew 5:37, NIV)

The Bible teaches that we are to be consistent in what we are and in what we say. Let your "yes" mean something. Be the kind of person who will be listened to when you speak. Do not exaggerate the truth. Let your "no" be a "no" of conviction and integrity, not an idle word without substance.

This has serious implications in evangelism. When the time comes to share the plan of salvation with someone, you need authority in your testimony or witness that is backed up by your life. One close friend says it this way, "To be effective, a Christian's walk and talk must be the same."

While teaching as a guest professor at Columbia Bible College in Columbia, South Carolina, I exercised each day in the gym. After each workout, I would go to a nearby restaurant and order a health shake—a milkshake with some good fruit and wheat germ in it. At the end of the three-weeks' term, I told my waitress, Rhonda, how much I had appreciated her service and graciousness and that I would not be back.

"Oh," she said, "you aren't from South Carolina?"

"No." I replied, "I'm from Texas and will be going home at the end of this week."

"Well, what brought you to South Carolina?"

I had been praying for an opportunity to witness to her for two weeks, but the door had never seemed to open until now. I told Rhonda that I had been teaching the Bible at a nearby Christian college.

"You sure did ruin my sister!" she retorted.

"What happened to your sister?"

"She was a perfectly normal religious person who went to the military chapel on the base. Everything was fine in our home until my sister had what she called a born-again experience at an evangelistic meeting. It has literally ruined her; she is the most miserable person I know."

"Did she tell you she was miserable?"

Instead of answering my question, she continued, "I'll tell you how bad it is. She doesn't cuss anymore; she doesn't drink; she doesn't smoke; she won't even roller skate."

"Rhonda, that last one is carrying it a little too far, but has your sister told you that she is miserable?"

"No. In fact, she actually thinks she is happy! But she must be crazy. Nobody could be happy and live like that."

The feeling Rhonda had about her sister is typical of those who do not understand what happens in the life of a person who commits himself or herself to Jesus Christ. Such attitudes are quickly dispelled as the Holy Spirit uses your testimony and the Scriptures to enlighten their understanding. "I have chosen the faithful way; I have placed Thine ordinances before me." (Psalm 119:30)

I briefly shared with Rhonda the biblical story of Mary and Martha, explaining that her sister, like Mary, had simply chosen the better alternative in life. After a few moments of conversation, Rhonda began to cry. Her obvious deep need gave me the opportunity to share the plan of salvation. She sat down at the counter while I drew the Bridge Illustration on a napkin, and she received Christ as her Savior and Lord that day.

LOVING PATIENCE

One of my Pauls is a gracious theologian and evangelist from India, Dr. A. B. Masilamani. When he began preaching as a young man, people would not let him into their homes. Often he would stand in the dusty street preaching and teaching the Bible while his Hindu audience sat on the porches of their houses listening. As the Holy Spirit began to deal with the people of his city, they began inviting him to come into their front yards. Finally, they invited him to their front steps and even on to the front porches with them.

Many months went by before they honored him by inviting him into their homes. At first, the people sat in chairs while he sat on the floor. Today when Dr. Masilamani visits the homes of these former Hindus who have now come to know Jesus, they have him sit in the chair and they sit on the floor at his feet as he breaks the Bread of Life for them.

This dear man was willing to wait on God for results while persisting in bearing his witness. Because of his life, I have asked myself many times if I would be willing to stand patiently outside the gates in the dusty street and proclaim the gospel to people in their homes. Would I humble myself and continue to sit on the floor while others sat in comfortable chairs so that I might explain the Good News to them? Would I persist in trying to give these people the most valuable gift in life in spite of their continual rejection? This is the kind of question you must ask regarding family members and close friends whom you deeply love but who continually reject the goodness and grace of God. Remember that some who come slowly become the strongest disciples of all.

WHOLE-HEARTED COMMITMENT

Whole-heartedness has been a problem for the people of God across the centuries. A sad epitaph for one of Judah's kings reads, "And he did right in the sight of the LORD, yet not with a whole heart." (2 Chronicles 25:2) Amaziah was twenty-five when he became king in Jerusalem, and he reigned for twenty-nine years, but he lived a half-hearted life.

God forbid that an inscription like that be written over our lives. I do not want to come to the end of my life and have it said, "Billie Hanks was a good old boy. He loved God, but he only served God with half his heart. He did the right things but was constantly wishing that he were doing something else."

Whether you are a pastor, missionary or a layman, this tragic epitaph serves as a warning. Amaziah was in the will of God vocationally; he was king and that is what God wanted him to be. He was in the will of God geographically and chronologically; he was king in the right place at the right time. But he was half-hearted in his service to God. No sin, other than impurity, will more greatly hamper the work of evangelism than a half-hearted, lukewarm commitment to Christ. "I know your deeds, that you are neither cold nor hot; I would that you were cold or hot. So because you are lukewarm, and neither hot nor cold, I will spit you out of My mouth." (Revelation 3:15, 16)

God desires our whole-hearted enthusiastic commitment to doing His will. If half-heartedness is considered average in the life of your church, then your positive example can be God's way of breathing new life and spiritual vitality into the fellowship. Paul Harvey puts it this way, "To be average is to be the best of the lousy or the lousiest of the best." God does not want you to be an average layman; He does not want you to be an average missionary; He does not want you to be an average Christian. He wants you to be a man or woman of God who is totally sold out to Him—and that's not average.

Your witness will abound as the wellspring of your relationship with God overflows from your life. James said, "Draw near to God and He will draw near to you." (James 4:8) That promise remains eternally true. If you have never had the privilege of leading someone to Christ, drink deeply from the living waters of His Word. Make up your mind to be usable right now, then pray and take the necessary practical steps to develop a godly character. Hide the six major verses on the plan of salvation in your heart (see Chapter 7), so you will be able to share them. Decide to be a positive witness. Determine not to live an average life.

CHAPTER 3

SHARING A WORD OF TRUTH

Over the years, I have found it helpful to categorize witnessing opportunities three ways. Just as a hammer, chisel and saw have three different functions related to carpentry, so there are three effective methods of witness related to evangelism. These approaches are:

1. Sharing a word of truth: briefly imparting a single truth about God (discussed in this chapter).
2. Sharing a testimony expressing the difference Christ has made in your life (Chapter 5).
3. Sharing the plan of salvation: explaining from Scripture how to come to know Christ personally (Chapter 7).

SHARING A WORD OF TRUTH

Sharing *a* word of truth (not the *entire* message of the gospel) means giving a casual, brief witness. It may be called a "wayside witness." It is usually brief, uncomplicated and something any Christian can do.

When my Discipler first began to train me in personal evangelism, he taught me to share the plan of salvation (approach 3). This presentation usually takes twelve to fifteen minutes. At first, I went around looking for people who had fifteen minutes to listen. However, sometimes there is not that much time available. If I couldn't find anyone with this much time, I assumed I wasn't supposed to witness.

When you are eager to share, it is frustrating not to be able to do it. So I went to my Discipler and said, "You know, it's wonderful that I've been able to lead some people to Christ, but there are dozens of people I meet every day to whom I could witness if I only knew how to do it in a shorter length of time."

He said, "Well, Billie, can't you just share a word of truth about Jesus Christ?"

"What do you mean?"

"Any true word about God is a witness," he replied. "You can just share a brief portion of the gospel. It doesn't have to be the entire plan of salvation."

This was a great relief to me because I had thought the only way to help people was to go from A to Z. I didn't realize that I could effectively witness in a less structured, informal manner.

The next week, my wife and I were driving to Uvalde, Texas. I was somewhat frustrated because we were running tight on time.

When we pulled into a service station, the young attendant grunted as he removed the gasoline cap and filled the tank. I soon discovered he had zero personality. I gave him my credit card and went inside to sign the ticket. As I was walking back out to the car, the Holy Spirit began to tug at my heart.

"Billie, I want you to share a word of truth with that man."

I hoped that I was talking to myself.

Reaching the car I asked my wife to pray for me, saying, "I believe the Lord wants me to witness to the station attendant."

She responded, "Honey, you don't have 15 minutes to spare." (She had learned the same method of witnessing I had.)

"I'm going to try a new way," I replied. "Just pray for me."

So I walked back into the station and looked at the young man. He was a big, strapping fellow, about eighteen or nineteen years old, and looked like half the football team of that little town. Having mustered up my courage, I prayed, "Lord, how do You want me to do this?"

I said, "Sir!"

He looked at me without saying a word.

"I want to tell you something. I have a message for you. God loves you very much, and has sent His Son, Jesus Christ, to die for you on the cross. He's been waiting for you to ask His Son into your heart so He can forgive your sins. He'd like to give you a wonderful life, but He won't force His way in. You'll have to pray and ask Him to come into your heart. The next step is yours. That's the message I'm supposed to deliver to you."

The young man never said a word. He stood there completely speechless. As he looked at me with a thoughtful expression on his face, I slowly walked back to the car. Out of curiosity, I turned around and looked through the window. He was still gazing at the wall where I'd been standing.

I drove off with real joy in my heart because I knew I had done what the Lord had wanted me to do. It wasn't the right time to open the Bible and show him all the verses, then pray with him. I was just supposed to share a word of truth. For the first time I was conscious of the Holy Spirit's empowering work in a three minute witness with a stranger.

THE EXAMPLE OF ANDREW

A word of truth is simply saying what you can about the Lord in a few brief words. Note Andrew's immediate desire after he met Jesus. "The first thing Andrew did was to find his brother Simon and tell him, 'We have found the Messiah!' (that is, the Christ)." (John 1:41, NIV) The author of this Gospel added the interpretation, but the words actually spoken by Andrew were these: "We have found the Messiah!"

These five words were probably the first witness Andrew shared with anyone. He had heard John the Baptist bear witness that Jesus was the Lamb of God. This occurred the day after the unforgettable experience when Andrew heard the voice of God saying, "This is my Son, whom I love; with Him I am well pleased" (Matthew 3:17, NIV), and watched the Holy Spirit descend like a dove as John baptized Jesus.

Andrew was convinced that the Messiah had come, and his witness was very simple. It was a word of truth: "We have found the Messiah!" Now why didn't he talk about the cross? Why didn't he mention the death, burial, and resurrection of Jesus? Why didn't he introduce the miracles and all the other components of the gospel? Because none of those things had yet happened. But he did say all that he knew and all that he could, for when a Jewish person says those five words, "We have found the Messiah," he has said it all.

Did his witness bear fruit?

Yes! Peter understood exactly what his brother said, and ultimately became one of the greatest Christians of all time. It all started with five simple words.

THE HOLY SPIRIT'S LEADING

God will begin to use you increasingly as you learn to share a word of truth anytime and every time He wants. As you mature, less and less prompting will be needed to motivate you in the direction of His will.

As a boy I owned an old but well trained cutting horse. When I began riding Midnight, I discovered that all I had to do was barely touch him with the reins on the side of his neck for him to turn in that direction.

That's the way God wants us to react in terms of witness. Wouldn't you like to be the kind of man or woman God could slightly touch with the leading of His Spirit, and you would immediately turn in the direction of His prompting? Witnessing would occur naturally and according to His will.

When you truly *desire* to be led in witnessing, God will give you a gentle, and soon familiar, touch of His Spirit. You will feel an inner urging to share a word of truth. Sometimes you may *not* feel impressed to witness, and that can be of God too. In trying to determine the leadership of the Holy Spirit in witnessing, simply ask, "Father, if this is not of You, take the impression away and leave me with no sense of guilt. But if it is of You Father, and You know that this person is ready and needs to be ministered to, and You want me to witness to him, then please impress it on me more firmly!

Make it so clear that I cannot miss Your leading."

The key to obedience is willingness to do God's will.

God has been faithful over the years to reveal His will when I was willing to do it. I have not always been sensitive to Him, and consequently, there've been some dismal failures.

One day at a car wash, I was waiting behind a lovely elderly woman driving one of the finest Cadillacs I have ever seen. She was elegantly dressed and her hair had a beautiful blue tint just like my grandmother's. She walked with a cane, but carried herself with great dignity. The Lord began to prompt me to witness, but I was apprehensive. If she had been a Japanese Sumo wrestler, I couldn't have been more afraid of her. I prayed, "Lord, is this impression to witness really of You? Please take it away if it is not of You, and press it on me harder if it is."

He deepened the impression. However, this elegant woman and I talked about the weather, about the gas mileage of her Cadillac, and about everything else except Jesus Christ. I just couldn't get myself to obey the Lord. I hesitated as if she would hit me with her cane if I mentioned Christ.

At the end of the line, with my car right behind hers, I had a thought. "I know, I'll get a tract for her out of my glove compartment." Though this might normally have been good, in my case it was a copout. I received this fleeting thought from God. "Go ahead and just talk to her about Me."

But I waited too long and she left. I knew I had failed. I had been disobedient to the Lord. Perhaps I would be the last Christian to have a chance to share Christ with her.

So I jumped in my car and started after her, never quite catching up. Finally as she neared a beautiful residential section, I was stopped by a traffic light and lost her completely. I spent half an hour driving around the area looking for her car.

Finally, in frustration, I pulled over to the side of the road, and broke down and cried. I said, "God, how long does it take for You to get a man to the place where You can trust him? How many times do I have to relearn to listen to you? When will You ever be able to trust me? God, please forgive me."

Claiming His forgiveness (1 John 1:9), I asked Him to send a more dedicated and faithful Christian to witness to that woman.

In the Christian life, you grow and you stumble and you fall and you get up—and sometimes you stumble and fall again. You have to *choose* to be usable on a daily basis. That has been my experience in witnessing. But every time you have a disheartening experience like the one above, God can use it to make you stronger, more sensitive and more careful to take advantage of the next opportunity.

A NEW UNDERSTANDING OF TIME

Time can be an obstacle in doing's God will if we do not understand that He purchased all the minutes of our life on Calvary. What if Philip had been too busy to obey God on the day when the Ethiopian eunuch was searching the Scriptures? (Acts 8:26-39)

Perhaps thousands or even millions of wonderful people are missing Christ today simply because Christians' priorities are out of line with God's will. Those who want to be used by God must be willing to do the unusual. Each year is studded with adventurous memories when you ask God for the daily opportunity to witness. Sometimes He will say *no* to that prayer. On other occasions, He will tell you to *wait*. But there will be many times when you will receive a clear and unmistakable *yes*.

After spending Christmas with the Grady Wilsons in North Carolina, my wife and I were flying home to Fort Worth. We had a scheduled stop in Atlanta. The Atlanta airport is the crossroads of the South, and well-known for the long distance to departure gates.

We ate at the Dobbs House restaurant thinking we had plenty of time. But the service was slow, and suddenly it was nearly time to take the long walk to our Texas-bound plane. Just as I began to feel it was time to leave the restaurant, I noticed a soldier sitting by himself at an adjacent table.

Humanly speaking, I did not want to become concerned about him because I didn't have time, but the Lord impressed him on my heart.

I thought, "No way, Lord. Please! You know I don't have the time right now. Surely this is just my own mind thinking I should witness to this man." So I prayed, "Lord, take this impression away if it isn't of You." then added, "I'll give him a tract. How would that be?"

Reaching into my briefcase, I pulled out a tract. But the Holy Spirit checked me in my spirit, saying, "No, he is not to receive a tract but your witness."

Returning the tract to my briefcase, I told my wife, "Honey, I am supposed to go talk to that soldier. There is no way we can catch our plane, but I am sure the Lord wants me to speak to him. You get on the plane and go to Dallas, and I'll catch the next flight. There's probably a flight every two hours or so."

She replied, "Great!"

Imagine a woman like that! I was so proud to have that kind of wife! She continued, "I'll get on the plane and pray that the Lord will bless your witness."

I turned around and looked at the large, tough-looking sergeant. Walking over to his table, I feebly began with, "Sir, are you from Texas?"

"Nope." he answered curtly.

I didn't know where to go from there, but the direct approach is often the best. So I said, "Well, Sir, the truth of the matter is that I have an important message for you and I am supposed to deliver it."

He said, "You are?"

"Yes, Sir. God sent me to speak to you."

"Who?" He was immediately interested. "Pull up a chair and tell me what He wants you to say."

I sat down, looked at him, and said, "He told me to tell you that He loves you, and that He sent His Son to die for you because He really does care about you. He wants to forgive and cleanse you from your sins. He has a place for you in heaven and He wants you to ask Jesus Christ to come into your heart. He wants you to become a real Christian."

Briefly I shared a little bit of my dad's testimony with him because he looked to be in his mid-forties, and my father gave his life to Christ when he was forty-six.

After a few minutes, I asked, "Would you like to become a Christian?"

"Yep!" he replied.

I thought, "Hey, this is too easy." then said, "Are you sure you want to become a Christian? It really costs to give your life to Christ." It scared me that he had said "OK" so quickly.

He looked at me sternly, and in a deep voice said, "Son, I don't say anything that I don't mean."

I answered, "Yes, Sir! Do you know how to pray?"

He said, "No, but you can teach me, can't you?"

I liked the way he got right to the point. I said, "Yes, Sir, I can teach you. I will lead you in a prayer, but you must pray it from your heart."

Assuming he would pray softly after me, I began, "Lord, I am a sinner."

No sooner had I said that than I heard a loud, deep voice, "LORD, I AM A SINNER!"

I opened my eyes and saw a startled waitress listening to what he was saying, and people at nearby tables looking in our direction. So I spoke more softly, "But I am sorry for my sins."

"BUT I AM SORRY FOR MY SINS," boomed the sergeant.

By the time we were through, some fifteen people around us had inadvertently become aware of his earnest prayer, and that man was gloriously saved. He knew clearly what he was doing. He said, "Thank you, Son. This is what I have wanted all my life. Thank you for showing me how to do it."

How long had this witness taken? Only a few minutes. I was even able to run down the long concourse and catch my plane—on time.

It's a small matter for God to hold a plane, speed up a plane, cancel a flight, or anything else He wants to do. Our part in the divine drama is simply to listen and obey. Once He can trust us in small matters, He will enlarge the area of our usefulness. The adventure grows and lives are changed as His love flows through our witness by the power of His Spirit. Boredom is incompatible with evangelism, because sharing Christ becomes life's greatest and most exciting experience. Time takes on a new meaning.

DEALING WITH PROBLEMS

1. *Victory over prayerless evangelism.* In the experience of most Christians who desire to witness, there will come the need to distinguish between witnessing out of a sense of obligation, and witnessing out of a sense of the Holy Spirit's leading. It should be as natural for a Christian to witness as it is for a river to flow. Specific prayer is the key to learning when and how your witness is to be given.

I once heard about a businessman who experienced anxiety when flying on airplanes because he knew that in all likelihood those he sat next to would not be born-again believers. And if his plane should crash, he would be the last person able to lead that man or woman to Christ. The responsibility was so enormous, it weighed him down and he became discouraged. At that point in his Christian experience, he had not learned the important role of prayer in determining God's will concerning sharing a witness in every situation.

In witnessing, unwarranted pressure is usually the result of failing to pray and, under God's leadership, appropriating the power of the Holy Spirit. We must not assume prerogatives that belong to Him. It is not our job to decide to whom we are going to witness. It is not even our job to be successful in witnessing. Our responsibility is to consistently remain in the position where we are sensitive to God's leading so we can be obedient, allowing the Holy Spirit to live and speak through us. It is our daily prayer to be made usable and our desire to share Christ that will make us ready for every God-given opportunity.

Before boarding a certain flight, I specifically prayed about the person who would sit next to me. It is a rewarding practice to pray for divine appointments during each day, God-given opportunities to witness. On this trip, the person next to me turned out to be a teenage boy about fifteen or sixteen. I prayed, "Lord, if You want me to witness to this boy, I am eager and ready, but let me know it is Your will by letting it come about naturally."

Taking my Scripture memory material out, I began to review my memory verses. As I was studying them, the boy looked over to see what I was doing, but I didn't say anything. After a few minutes it just seemed natural to show him one of the verses and say, "Can you explain that verse to me? Tell me what you think it means."

He replied, "Sure, I'll be glad to."

He sat there for a long time studying the verse. Then he said, "OK, Mister, I'm ready," and he explained the meaning of the verse.

I said, "Great. You're right on target. Try this one."

Again he did well, so I gave him a third one. This one was on salvation.

He totally misunderstood its meaning. So I said, "Would you like for me to explain it?"

He replied, "Sure!"

Soon we were discussing the plan of salvation, and before the plane touched down in Denver, he had settled matters with Christ. It was totally natural and ended in peace and spontaneous joy!

2. *Victory over feelings of inadequacy.* This problem is often the result of a lack of knowledge of God's Word. A friend once talked to a business acquaintance about the fact that he didn't witness. Though successful in business and a leader in his community, he felt like a failure when his first witnessing opportunity ended in confrontation and unanswered questions. He had determined never to witness again until he felt confident in his ability to do it successfully.

You may have had a similar experience. If so, you are not alone in the school of evangelism. Such experiences simply underscore the need for discipline in the area of Bible study. Look for specific answers for the excuses you expect to encounter. The section on "Witnessing Helps" in *The Open Bible* is an excellent place to start learning how to skillfully respond to questions. Knowing the Word of God and how to present it will give you a great deal of security and additional effectiveness.

3. *Victory over fear.* I have never met a Christian who has not experienced the element of fear in witnessing. Fear diminishes as you gain experience, but it never completely goes away. Fear is just an advanced form of timidity, and it can be used positively in our lives if it reminds us that the Holy Spirit must be the One to do the work. Like a little red light that blinks, the Holy Spirit continually

reminds us, "Depend on Me! Depend on Me!" The Lord will give boldness, confidence, and freshness, making witnessing increasingly natural as you apply what you learn experientially.

Fear frequently is the result of failure to *appropriate* God's resources by faith. That is why Paul wrote to Timothy and said, "For God has not given us the spirit of fear, but of power, and of love and of a sound mind." (2 Timothy 1:7, KJV) The element that you need to understand in this verse is that God is the One who gives us soundness of mind, peace of heart and the power to minister. Fear is definitely not from God, but He can use it to remind you of your need for Him. As the psalmist says, "When I am afraid, I will trust in You." (Psalm 56:3, NIV)

By faith you must determine to develop spontaneity and overcome fear by carrying out Peter's admonition: "Always be prepared to give an answer to everyone who asks you to give the reason for the hope that you have." (1 Peter 3:15, NIV) If you are prepared in your working knowledge of the Scriptures, fear ceases to be a significant problem. Instead, the small amount that remains serves only as a helpful reminder to trust in the Holy Spirit's power rather than your knowledge of the Bible.

CHAPTER 4

INTERCESSION

Years ago while I was ministering in another country, a very concerned woman and her daughter waited outside the church building to talk with me at the close of a service. The mother explained that her husband, a prominent businessman in the area, was a hardened agnostic. He felt no need in his life for God and basically worshipped his possessions and his good health. I assured them that I would join them in the prayer that God would bring him to see the need for the Savior. As we talked, I recalled the verse which says, "...if two of you agree on earth about anything that they may ask, it shall be done for them by My Father who is in heaven." (Matthew 18:19)

Unexpectedly, the lady's husband arrived in his new black Cadillac, a rarity in that part of the world, where American cars were extremely scarce. His erect bearing, expensive black leather jacket, and muscular build accented an egotistical spirit.

His wife introduced us but made a classic mistake by saying something like, "Honey, I have asked this gentleman to pray for you." I could almost see his mind working: "This man is a complete stranger. Why do I need *his* prayers? And furthermore, what do I need, anyway?"

Though I hoped my face didn't show it, I wanted to find the nearest rock and crawl under it! Quickly and silently I prayed, "Father, what do I do now? If he asks me to pray, what should I request?"

After an awkward silence, the man replied, "Sure. Everybody could use a little prayer now and then." Polite sarcasm tinged his response.

Almost instantly, my prayer for guidance was answered. The Holy Spirit reminded me to intercede for him by praying against his two most obvious areas of idolatry. If his money and good health were keeping him from seeing his need for Christ, they were his enemies rather than blessings. I was a little afraid when the Lord told me what to pray, because the prayer was unusual and specific, and because it could easily be misunderstood.

For these reasons, I looked directly into his eyes and very slowly and purposefully said, "Sir, I do not believe you want me to pray for you, because God has already told me what to pray for, and I don't think you are going to like it."

With a little less sarcasm, he replied, "No, I want you to pray for me."

I warned him again that he would not like what I was going to request. I further explained that he could be sure the prayer would be answered because the Lord had specifically told me what to ask for.

As we talked, the expressions on the faces of his wife and daughter indicated how earnestly they expected God to guide our conversation and to convict him of his need. Encouraged, I said, "All right, let's pray." He answered, "You mean, right now?" I said, "Yes, if we're going to do it, let's do it now."

We bowed our heads, and I felt that deep assurance and authority that God provides at such moments. "Father," I prayed, "in the name of Your Son Jesus Christ, in order that this man might know that there is a God in heaven who is real and who answers prayer, and that he might come to realize his need of the Savior, please let him go bankrupt six months from today and be flat on his back in the hospital when that occurs. When these things come to pass, please let him understand that they are for his good and a sign that You love him. Amen."

As we opened our eyes and raised our heads, he sarcastically said, "Thanks!" But almost simultaneously a joyful affirmation and "Amen" came from the lips of his wife and daughter. I can scarcely remember greater evidence of selfless love! They were willing to lose everything in order that he might be convicted of his sin.

About eight weeks later, a thrilling letter arrived at our home in Texas. The man's teenage daughter recounted the events of the two-month period. Her father was plagued by sleepless nights. How would he pay his hospital bills when he was bankrupt? And how could he earn money while sick in bed? Feverishly, he attempted to hide money to pay for his coming medical expenses. God had gotten his full attention!

He was experiencing what the Bible calls conviction of sin. Such treatment may seem harsh and such a prayer unloving, until one stops to realize that God isn't broke and both funds and good health can easily be restored if and when He feels it is in our best interest.

The girl's letter was literally an epistle of *joy* as she described her father's conversion and acceptance of Christ. After years of indifference, he had been jolted into attending a nearby church eight times in two months. On the eighth visit, he finally admitted his need, abandoned his defenses, and committed his life to the Savior.

At this point, people typically ask, "What happened four months later? Did God take away his money and his health?" He would have, exactly on schedule, but the man gave his resources and his health to God on the night that he became a Christian.

When our idolatry ceases and we begin to seek the kingdom of God, the very things which were enemies to our heavenly Father become tools for good in His hands. Let me illustrate.

Years later as I related this experience during a Bible conference in another country, a missionary stood to his feet in the middle of the service. He said, "May I finish your story?" and proceeded to tell us what had happened to that same man in subsequent years.

He reported how the man had grown spiritually and become a widely known, respected Christian leader in his country. He frequently used his black Cadillac to assist the Prime Minister by picking up visiting dignitaries at the airport. While driving them to their destination, he would share his testimony and express his gratitude and love for Christ. The very symbol of his alienation from God became a means of serving Him.

PRAYING FOR THE LOST

The previous story illustrates praying for conviction of sin. This is the easiest kind of intercession and is probably the best place to start. You can intercede for others with great boldness and confidence when you ask the Holy Spirit to convict lost people who are unbelieving and saved people who are living in spiritual compromise. When explaining the basis for this powerful kind of prayer, Jesus once said that when the Holy Spirit comes He will "convict the world concerning sin." (John 16:8b)

The whole point of intercessory prayer is asking God *to do what He already desires to accomplish.* Conviction of sin is clearly His will, and He will always honor our prayers when we make that request. Pause to consider the implications. Imagine what could happen if we begin to ask for conviction of sin in the lives of those around us.

God is patiently waiting for us to pray for conviction. He is waiting for us to agree with Him about the light and the spiritual help He wants to bring into the lives of those in darkness. Jesus was called the "light of the world," but the Scriptures say that "men loved the darkness rather than the light; for their deeds were evil...everyone who does evil hates the light, and does not come to the light, lest his deeds should be exposed. But he who practices the truth comes to the light, that his deeds may be manifested as having been wrought in God." (John 3:19b-21) The result of our intercession is that God illuminates the hearts of those for whom we pray so they can see and forsake whatever keeps them in spiritual darkness.

Although some prayers are answered immediately, intercession often requires patience. Consider a puzzle. Individual pieces have to wait until the pattern begins to form. Only when finished can we see the whole. God alone can see each event which must come to pass in order for Him to bless us as He answers our prayers.

As God's children, we are given glimpses of His great plans, but even then, *patience* is required. We must remember that "with the Lord one day is as a thousand years, and a thousand years as one day." (2 Peter 3:8) Our concept of time has little significance to God. What matters to Him is faith, truth, love, and character. These aspects of life have lasting value, but they are developed slowly. When you pray, you must be careful to "let patience have its perfect work, that you may be perfect and complete, lacking nothing." (James 1:4, NKJV)

PRAYING FOR THE SICK

Another form of intercession deals with praying for physical health. James says, "Is anyone among you sick? Let him call for the elders of the church, and let them pray over him, anointing him with oil in the name of the Lord." (James 5:14)

This kind of intercession is in some ways more difficult to practice than praying for the lost. The Scriptures make it clear that God "is patient...not wishing for any to perish but for all to come to repentance." (2 Peter 3:9b) His will is not so obvious with regard to physical health. He *always* wants the spiritually sick to be healed, but it is *not* always His purpose for the physically sick to be healed. When praying for someone to be convicted of sin, you know God's will in advance, but when you pray for someone who is sick, this is not the case. There are those whom God wills to heal, and those whom He does not.

WHEN HEALING IS GOD'S WILL

To pray effectively for someone who is sick, first analyze your own spiritual condition. Does your prayer come from a *clean* heart? The Scripture says, "Confess your sins to one another, and pray for one another, so that you may be healed." (James 5:16a) Is your prayer offered in the calm assurance that God is able to answer it? The Scripture says, "The prayer offered in faith will restore the one who is sick." (James 5:15a) This is the kind of intercession that is experienced when the conditions of *personal purity* and *faith* are present in the lives of those who are making the request and it is specifically the Father's will to restore the person's health. On such occasions we are privileged to offer what James calls "effective prayer"—the kind that comes when a righteous man seeks God's will in faith. This is the intercession that accomplishes much (James 5:16b).

A mature understanding of this teaching should lead every Christian to take continual inventory of his walk with God. Why? Because if things are not morally, ethically, and spiritually right in your life, the effectiveness of your prayers will be hindered and you will be powerless. Let's assume, however, that you have both purity and faith, but your intercession for the healing of a friend or loved one is still answered with a "no." This leads us to the second category of intercession for healing.

WHEN HEALING IS NOT GOD'S WILL

Several years ago, as a guest speaker at a college in California, I met an unforgettable young man. Jerry was born with an abnormal bodily formation. He has little stumps for arms, and one foot attached to the middle of his torso. He travels in a motorized wheelchair.

A close friend, who is a professor on that campus, told me about the ministry Jerry carries out on the college parking lot. He loves kids and stacks them on his wheelchair, driving it about as they scream with delight. He allows no one to feel sorry for him and is obviously happier than many of the physically normal people on campus who are handicapped in other ways.

His roving wheelchair is unmistakable, because it displays bumper stickers like "God Loves You" and "Praise the Lord!" Popularly known as a person who is excited about Christ, Jerry ministers in a unique fashion by wearing a bootie on his foot which he calls a "Wordless Book." Each toe is knit in a different color. As he points at the gold toe, he explains its meaning: "God is the ruler of heaven, and He wants you to know Him and experience His love." The next toe is dark, so he explains the problem of sin.

Curiously the neighborhood children ask about the red toe, and he tells them how Christ shed His blood for their sins. Pointing to the white toe, he continues: "That's what Christ wants to do in your life: He desires to enter your heart and make you clean by forgiving your sins." By the last toe, which is green, they are spellbound as he tells them how God wants them to grow spiritually and become productive in the lives of others. Kids eat it up!

My friend and I do not know if God has led faithful Christians to ask that He heal Jerry and provide his missing limbs. We do know, however, that God is totally aware of Jerry's circumstances. It is also safe to assume that people of faith know Jerry, care about his condition, and would *eagerly* join in asking for such a miracle if God ever prompted them to do so.

If this is true, why would God allow Jerry to be left with his body? The very fact that he is different, sets him apart and gives him the platform from which he bears his powerful witness for Christ.

Jerry demonstrates his faith on a daily basis; therefore, his physical condition does not indicate a lack of faith on his part, nor is it a reflection upon the faith of others. Once this is understood, our thoughts immediately turn from *pity* to *privilege*. What a compliment it is to Jerry that God would see within him the strength and character needed to carry out the sacred and challenging task to which he has been called. Jerry reminds me of the apostle Paul who, though pure and strong in faith, lived with a physical infirmity which made him more usable for God's glory.

Physical illness needs to be positively understood. Although the Lord raised Lazarus from the dead, later He also allowed him to die a second time. The Scriptures do not tell us how he died, but we assume that an illness was probably responsible. The same is true of every other person whom Christ healed or brought back to life during His earthly ministry.

Why did God allow them to die again? Because since the time of Adam, His plan has been to share heaven with those who have believed in Him and placed their faith in His Son. Jesus said, "Let not your heart be troubled; believe in God, believe also in Me. In My Father's house are many dwelling places; if it were not so, I would have told you; for I go to prepare a place for you. And if I go and prepare a place for you, I will come again, and receive you to

Myself; that where I am, there you may be also." (John 14:1-3)

Do not for one moment think that Lazarus, who had already experienced heaven for four days, yearned to return and continue living here on earth. His attitude was probably more like that of the apostle Paul, who said, "I am hard-pressed from both directions, having the desire to depart and be with Christ, for that is very much better; yet to remain on in the flesh is more necessary for your sake." (Philippians 1:23 & 24)

The only reason Lazarus, Paul, or any other Christian would want to stay on earth would be for the sake of the ministry and for fellowship with those family members and people whom they love. Beyond that, the new body we will receive, the glorious union with Christ, the fellowship with the departed saints who have gone before us, and the joys of heaven itself make death the closest friend of every believer. Without death, we could not shed the frailties of this life or receive the wonders that await us in the kingdom Christ has prepared on our behalf.

Because accidents account for the deaths of only a few, it is sickness which God most often uses to fulfill His will in our lives and bring us into the kingdom of heaven. Those who fear death need to be reminded that the grave has lost its victory and death has lost its sting (1 Corinthians 15:55-57). There is nothing to be feared in going to sleep and waking up in the presence of the Savior.

If it were not for death, the billions who have lived in the world's history would have overpopulated the earth and turned it into a hellish existence with no escape. Christ has taken man's worst enemy and used it for a higher purpose.

Intercession must never be thought of as trying to persuade God to do something He really does not want to do. It is not an effort to corner Him in a theological box where certain verses are used to make Him perform according to our will, rather than His. Your objective is to *agree* with Him and to claim those things which please Him, even though they may cut straight across the grain of your human nature. Of course you hate to lose a loved one or see a young man handicapped like Jerry, but be careful to listen as you pray. If God speaks to you as He did to Paul and the answer is "no," by faith be prepared to praise Him as much as if the answer were "yes." You can afford to do this, because He knows what is best for you and no request which you bring to Him as His child will ever go unheard or unanswered.

JESUS THE INTERCESSOR

As you read your Bible, you will soon become aware that the Lord Jesus lived a life of intercession. His petitions were always directed toward the needs of those He loved. He never asked for a palace, a chariot or an extensive wardrobe for Himself, as is evidenced by the fact that He didn't have them. He came into the world to seek and save the lost (Luke 19:10), and He left the world to prepare a heavenly home for those same people. His whole life was spent seeking benefit for others. He lived and breathed intercession. Even on the cross, He interceded for sinners of all the ages when He uttered this prayer in pain: "Father, forgive them; for they do not know what they are doing." (Luke 23:34a)

We are given a glimpse into Jesus' early ministry of intercession when, speaking to the twelve, He turned His attention to Simon Peter, saying, "Simon, Simon, Satan has asked to sift you as wheat. But I have prayed for you...that your faith may not fail. And when you have turned back, strengthen your brothers." (Luke 22:31, NIV)

It was Christ's prayer that restored Peter to useful service after his darkest hour. It was intercession that helped Peter come to true repentance after he had denied the Lord Jesus Christ three times. In his own testimony, written many years later, he said, "The Lord knows how to rescue the godly from temptation." (2 Peter 2:9a) Paul brings this into focus for us today when he declares, "No temptation has overtaken you but such as is common to man; and God is faithful, who will not allow you to be tempted beyond what you are able, but with the temptation will provide the way of escape also, that you may be able to endure it." (1 Corinthians 10:13)

Jesus' longest and best-known personal prayer is found in the seventeenth chapter of John. Lifting His eyes toward heaven, His prayer was characterized by words like these: "I ask on their behalf;" (John 17:9) and "My prayer is not for them alone. I pray also for those who will believe in Me." (John 17:20, NIV)

He continued by beseeching the Father not to take us out of this world but to keep us away from the influence of Satan. His prayer was consistent with His emphasis that Christians should live in the world but not be *like* it (John 17:15-16).

Jesus' intercession for the disciples intensified as He came toward the close of His earthly ministry. He was leaving His devoted followers behind, and He knew they would face trials and temptations with the potential of overwhelming their faith. To prepare them for the hard times to come, He told them about the future: "They will put you out of the synagogue; in fact, a time is coming when anyone who kills you will think he is offering a service to God." (John 16:2)

In his deep concern that they not feel deserted during His time of persecution, He told them of a Helper He would send to be with them in the near future (John 15:26). He promised that this Helper would bear witness to His divinity (John 16:14), recall His teachings to their remembrance (John 14:26), guide them (John 16:13), disclose the future to them (John 16:14), explain the truths of God (John 16:15), and convict the world concerning sin, righteousness and judgment (John 16:8). As the result of His intercession (Romans 8:26), this Helper, the Holy Spirit, would come to indwell and empower them to be His witnesses beginning in Jerusalem and finally to the remotest parts of the earth (Acts 1:8).

After the Lord ascended to heaven, His ministry of intercession continued. He simply changed His location! Upon His departure, "Christ did not enter a holy place made with hands, a mere copy of the true one, but into heaven itself, now to appear in the presence of God for us." (Hebrews 9:24) The writer of Hebrews goes on to explain that Christ "always lives to make intercession" (Hebrews 7:25c) for us and "...is able to save forever those who draw near to God *through Him*." (Hebrews 7:25a, b)

Without Christ interceding for us, there would be no hope for the human race. Why is this true? Isaiah expressed it in these dramatic words: "All our righteous acts are like filthy rags." (Isaiah 64:6, NIV) They are a stench in the nostrils of a holy God. Paul said, "There is none righteous, no, not one." (Romans 3:10, KJV) Without Christ's many prayers on our behalf and His selfless act of intercession when He took our place on the cross, we would be doomed to the penalty we deserve because of our sin. How eternally grateful we can be that Christ cared enough to pray and give Himself on our behalf. He was the perfect intercessor!

Interceding for others is the most *Christlike, unselfish* praying that you and I will ever do. It includes praying for the lost and praying for the saved, praying for the sick and praying for the well. It reaches out in faith and affects the lives of people next door and in the remotest part of the world. It is urgent, yet patient. And above all else, it seeks the will of God in every situation.

CHAPTER 5

SHARING YOUR TESTIMONY

Beyond "sharing a word of truth," the second method of evangelism is learning to give an effective personal testimony. This means telling why, when, where, and how you came to know Christ as your Lord and Savior.

We see this pattern in the life of the apostle Paul. On one occasion he was brought before King Herod Agrippa II, an Idumean king appointed by the Romans over the Jews. "Agrippa said to Paul, 'You have permission to speak for yourself.' So Paul motioned with his hand and began his defense." (Acts 26:1, NIV) Paul responded to this opportunity by sharing his own experience with Christ (Acts 26:2-29).

In this instance, Paul didn't merely share a word of truth. He gave a lengthy, detailed testimony of what God had done in his life. Often, sharing what God has done in our own lives can communicate more effectively than any other form of witness. This basic approach to evangelism involves a little more time and frequently requires earning a hearing. Paul earned a hearing with Agrippa by identifying with him. He started out by complimenting him, then told him that because of his background, he would be able to understand what Paul was about to say. Soon the king was listening intently.

DIFFERENT KINDS OF TESTIMONIES

We can give many different kinds of personal testimonies in addition to our conversion experience. Actually, we have a new and different testimony each week of our Christian lives. You may say, "Well, I have just one testimony, because I was saved just once."

This is true concerning salvation, but every time God answers prayer, you have a new testimony. Maybe you have been sick and God healed you in answer to the prayers of your family and friends. You may have had financial problems which God solved in a miraculous way. You may have had a difficult interpersonal relationship that God reconciled, or perhaps had major difficulties in your own family that God overcame.

Every one of the above situations gives you a new testimony to share with other people—believers and unbelievers alike. Time after time, God has been faithful, giving you new evidence to share of His grace, mercy, and love. Every day, every week, every month, every year, He demonstrates His adequacy. But the testimony God typically uses most effectively in evangelism has to do with your conversion.

YOUR CONVERSION TESTIMONY

The most important element of a conversion testimony is telling *why* you became a Christian. Why did you decide to become a follower—a disciple – of Jesus Christ? Think of one word that would state as clearly as possible the reason why you became a Christian. Maybe it happened because of conviction...fear...or loneliness. You could have become aware of the love of God or of the reality of divine judgment. You may have made your decision for any of a hundred different reasons.

When you share your testimony with others, tell them what you have experienced and seek to identify honestly with their weaknesses and needs. If you have felt fear, tell them. If you have been lonely, tell them. If you felt alienated from God and became bitter, share that. If you were confused and frustrated and could not understand why there were wars, accidents, famines, and prejudice, say so.

One of the most powerful tools you have to help others is the ability to aid them in understanding why you as a person of this century decided to give your life to someone who lived 2,000 years ago. They must be led to see that your help and inner joy have not come from discovering a new cause or a religious code of ethics, but from a relationship with a vital, living Person, who is eternal. They must understand that you have committed your life to Him on the basis of who He is and what He did on our behalf.

God allowed us to see His face and sinless character in the person of Jesus Christ so we would desire to know Him personally. This is why He became a man, lived a perfect life before us, and demonstrated His love on the Cross and His power in the Resurrection. Above all, people must be helped to realize the truth that Jesus is God, that they are important to Him, and that His call demands a response.

Why is the issue of *why* being emphasized so much? Because people are interested in knowing why. They do not necessarily want to know *how* you became a Christian. This is not their primary concern. Yet this is what most of us normally tell them. When we are asked to give our testimony, we often say, "I became a Christian at the age of such and such." That tells people *when* we became Christians. Then we go on to tell that it happened in such and such a revival meeting or in a certain location. That is *where* we became Christians.

But the important thing most people want to know is *why* you placed your faith in Him and what He has done for you. In essence, they want to know how He has affected the quality of your life.

WHAT TO EMPHASIZE

In sharing your testimony, there are some occasions when you should not emphasize *when* you were converted. If I were talking to a man in his forties about Jesus Christ, I would not tell him that I was saved at the age of ten, because he would not identify with my experience. Satan does everything he can to discount your testimony, and telling a forty-year-old man of a childhood conversion helps him to do so. That man might think something like this: "Aha! That boy was educated into Christianity. He didn't have a real experience with God—it was just a psychological or educational process. The boy grew up in a Christian home and went to Sunday school and church, so how can I be sure something really happened to change his life?"

A man who is forty may have become reasonably cynical. He may have seen immaturity, bickering or hypocrisy in the lives of some church members.

We need to pray that God will help us give our testimonies to different people in the way that will most clearly identify with their need. We must think through what parts of our testimony they most need to hear.

When should you tell people *when* you were converted? If you were sharing your testimony with someone in his fifties, and you came to Jesus when you were forty-five, it would be appropriate to do so. An older adult will be able to identify with the experience of another older adult. He might say something like this to himself, "Well, if you found Christ at this age, and have had a change in your life because of faith in Him, maybe I can too."

I have a good friend who was converted at the age of sixty and feels that he has to make up for lost time. In his witnessing experiences, he generally shares with people who are younger. His approach sounds something like this: "Frank, I pray you won't have to wait as long as I did to find the truth. I hope you won't make the same mistake I made. If I had only made this commitment at age forty, what a difference it would have made in my life!"

In sharing our testimonies, there are times when we do say when we were converted and times when we don't. The same is true for *where* we were converted. Sometimes we should mention the location of our conversion; sometimes we should not.

To illustrate this, let's assume that I am a dedicated Christian factory worker about forty-five years of age. I want to share Christ with one of my fellow workers at the factory who is pretty miserable. He is a nice, moral person, but he is lost. He doesn't know Christ, and if he were to die, he would not go to heaven. This has burdened me deeply while we have been working together for over a year.

I happen to know that Jack, my co-worker, likes to fish. Since I am a fisherman, too, I've taken the opportunity to ask him to go fishing with me, hoping to be able to share with him what he really needs most in his life—Jesus Christ. Now, imagine that we are fishing, and I will illustrate witnessing *incorrectly* and then *correctly*.

WITNESSING INCORRECTLY

Late on Friday afternoon we arrive at my favorite fishing place and launch the boat. It has been a beautiful afternoon, and the sunset is gorgeous. We are planning to fish into the night.

We aren't out there very long before I say, "Jack, it sure is great to be out here fishing with you. You know, I've been looking forward to getting together so we can talk."

He thought my purpose was fishing, but I have indicated a different purpose before my worm is even wet!

I continue, "Jack, I have been looking forward to asking you if you have ever made a personal commitment to Jesus Christ. Have you ever given your life to Christ, Jack?"

He answers, "No, I don't suppose I have." I may use all the right religious words, and he may listen out of courtesy.

"Well, Jack, I want to talk to you about that for a few minutes. I would like to tell you that Jesus Christ is wonderful. I gave my life to Him five years ago."

"I visited a little white church building near our home in Louisiana, and an evangelist preached a powerful message. The organ and the piano began to play 'Just As I Am,' the invitation was given to come forward, and Louise and I gave our lives to Christ. He has been the greatest discovery of my life, Jack, and I would like to challenge you to give your life to Christ as well."

Now all of this may be correct and true, but it may be irrelevant to Jack's need. I haven't told him *why* I became a Christian—only when, how and where. Now let's look at a better approach.

WITNESSING CORRECTLY

You are out in the boat together, and you notice that the sunset is simply fantastic. Most people like the outdoors and its beauty. You look up from your fishing and say, "Jack, this is great. It's so peaceful and quiet this evening. Look at that sunset. It's more beautiful than any stained-glass window I've seen."

What is Jack's mental association when you say "stained-glass window"? With church, most likely, for you have helped him into that mindset. Now the difference between this approach and the previous one is that in the first, I took him out of the boat and mentally moved him across the country to Louisiana, where there is a little white church building. I had him waiting for an invitation— a custom with which he probably wasn't familiar. I mentioned a hymn he had never heard and a term, "evangelist," with which he was not familiar.

In the second approach, you're keeping him right in that boat with you. When you comment on the beauty of the sunset reminding you of the colors of a stained-glass window, he agrees.

So you say, "I am always amazed when I realize God can make a world this beautiful." Just about everyone believes in God and thinks the world is a nice place to live. You are on safe ground here.

"Yeah." He answers.

Then you may change the subject for awhile. When Jesus said, "I will make you fishers of men," (Matthew 4:19, NIV) He meant just that. Just as we have to be taught the art of fishing, Christians have to learn the art of witnessing and sharing our testimonies so we can be of help to others. A good fisherman never attempts to set the hook until the fish actually strikes. He has to be patient. When a fish takes the bait, you allow him to run with the line and reel him in slowly.

After having fished awhile, you resume your conversation. You know Jack and his wife have a teenage son with whom they are having serious problems.

"Jack, you sure have a fine looking son. How is he doing in football?"

"We're proud of him," he replies. "We think he is going to make first string this year."

You reply, "Football was our son's number one love in high school. Those were fun years, but they were also some of the hardest for our family."

"How's that?"

"We almost lost communication at home. I guess we got too busy in our own worlds. Louise and I even began to feel the strain in our marriage. It got pretty bad for awhile."

Jack responds with a note of surprise. "I didn't think you and your wife ever had any problems."

"Well, we don't right now, but that wasn't true in the past. Even we were surprised how we worked them out."

"Really? What did you do?"

"We tried everything. We read books. We went to a marriage counselor and couldn't find the answers anywhere. So we decided to try something different. We weren't religious people, having only been to church three or four times in our married life. But one night, we knew that we had to find some answers or lose our marriage. That night we decided to do something we had never done before. We actually *prayed* together and asked for help."

"That was just a little step, but it seemed to make a difference. After that, we decided to give church an honest try. So we found one nearby and visited several times. Soon we realized the church was full of people just like us with similar problems, but they had found some real answers. After several weeks, we discovered that the real issue was giving our lives to Christ, not just attending church. I know this may sound overly simple, but it worked."

"For the past five years, Christ has made a profound difference in our lives. It took awhile, but our son Ron finally followed our lead. Now we have real happiness in our home, because we are all headed in the same new direction."

By this time, you have established an openness that will enable you to talk with Jack about how he too, can give his life to Christ and begin working on his problems.

SHARING CHRIST NATURALLY

Someone has said that Jesus' method of witnessing was super-naturally natural. Without a doubt, the major word that should typify our witness is *natural*. Whenever I hear someone beat the drum saying "Witness! Witness!" I become politely annoyed. This is comparable to a man standing by a riverbank shouting, "Flow, river, flow!" You don't need to tell a river to flow, because it does it naturally.

Do you like to talk about people you love? It's natural. That's why I like to tell about my wife and my daughters so much. I love them! A Christian who loves Jesus Christ will find it natural to talk about Him.

If a Christian is not witnessing and sharing his testimony with others, there is something basically wrong, or dammed up, in his Christian life. A spiritually healthy Christian will naturally witness, just as a river will naturally flow.

SCRIPTURE IN A TESTIMONY

We have dealt with why, when, where, and how. What about Scripture in your personal testimony? Frequently ignorance of the verses that explain the plan of salvation or unconfessed sin becomes the dam in a Christian's witnessing experience.

You should have appropriate Scripture verses built into your testimony. Be sure you have committed them to memory, because you will not always have your Bible with you when you have an opportunity to give a personal testimony.

THE NEED FOR HONESTY

One of my finest Timothys was a strong, husky young man who is now an evangelist. One day he offered to drive me from Fort Worth to Kerrville, Texas, where I was going to preach. I was physically fatigued at this time, and he was concerned I might have an auto accident on the way. He also knew that this would provide some one-to-one time for study and prayer.

As we were driving along, I asked him to give his testimony. I frequently do this with my Timothys to help them learn to share more effectively.

He said, "Billie, I don't have much of a testimony."

It bothers me to hear any Christian say that. To say you don't have much of a testimony when Jesus Christ saved you from hell and is preparing you for heaven is an unthinking statement. What he meant, of course, was that he'd never been a drug addict, robbed a bank, been immoral or spent time in jail. I'm glad he didn't have to go through all that to find Christ, but his forgiveness and new life are just as real as the apostle Paul's.

He said, "I was born into a Christian home and became a Christian early in life. Then God led me to a Christian college, where I surrendered for the ministry. There I met a Christian girl, fell in love, and married her. Then God led me to seminary, and now I am an evangelist."

In my own gentle way I looked at him and said, "You liar!"

He was startled. "What? Are you calling me a liar?"

"Why not? You just lied. Don't tell me that phoney story. I want to hear your true story." At times, when you are training someone, frankness is the need of the hour.

He looked at me as if shell-shocked. I didn't know what was going to happen next. I said, "Now, go ahead and give me your real testimony."

"It would embarrass me." he replied.

"Now, listen. Enough of this sugar-coated stuff. People want to know *why* you became a Christian. So tell them!"

"Well, if you must know, I was a chronic liar from the time I was a little child. My parents couldn't trust me. I couldn't even trust myself. From the time I was a little boy to the time I was converted, I could not tell the truth. I lied all the time."

"Now, I can believe that. That's a story I can handle."

This man had been afraid of being open and honest. The next week he preached in El Paso, Texas, and God led him to give his real testimony. A man in his forties came up to him at the end of the service and said, "Preacher, is what you just said the truth? About your being a habitual liar?"

He said, "Yes, Sir. I was one, and I couldn't help myself."

The man said, "If God could help you, maybe He could change me as well." And the man was converted that night.

Now, what if my Timothy had gotten up and given his usual, bland, incomplete testimony with that poor bleeding man sitting there?

The same need exists in your office, in your home, and in your school. People are hurting everywhere, but it doesn't help them to hear about your successes unless they also learn about your failures and how God dealt with them.

Always identify with weaknesses and needs as truthfully as you can, but don't overdo it. If you were immoral, just say that you have lived in immorality and avoid the details. You also don't have to pretend to understand a problem. Don't say, "I was almost a drug addict." when in reality, you were only taking aspirin. Lost people can spot a phoney. God is never glorified by the sin of exaggeration.

SUGGESTED ASSIGNMENT

Write out your personal testimony using the form on the following pages. Then begin praying for a meaningful opportunity to share it with someone this week. Remember the Lord's promise to give you power to witness through His indwelling Spirit (Acts 1:8). This simple exercise will help you think through your own testimony and prepare you to be used by God.

MY PERSONAL TESTIMONY

1.   My life before becoming a Christian.

2.   How I realized my need for Christ.

3.   Why I received Christ as my Lord and Savior.

4.   When and how I made that decision.

5. Specific ways Christ has changed my life since I became a Christian.

6. What the Lord is teaching me now.

CHAPTER 6

CONFESSION

Unconfessed sin is like spoiled food in the pantry, dirt in the living room, or anything else which degrades its surroundings. It is totally out of character with a redeemed life!

Because we are still imperfect even after our conversion experience, confession is the norm, but ever-increasing purity in thought and deed is our constant goal. Living in compromise with, or harboring sin in our hearts is unacceptable and unbecoming in God's children.

The sins of pride, lust, lying, bitterness, or a lack of faith, have the same negative effect on the life of a believer that they have on an unbeliever. However, there is one important exception: A Christian is assured of forgiveness and knows how to claim that promised help. The Bible says, "If we confess our sins, He is faithful and righteous to forgive us our sins, and to cleanse us from all unrighteousness." (1 John 1:9)

Unconfessed sin takes away the joy of our salvation and the dignity that accompanies a committed Christian's life. Lack of confession can be equated by a life of spiritual mediocrity, or what the Bible calls "carnality." It can produce depression, feelings of guilt, discouragement, lack of assurance, and a host of other symptoms which erode the wonderful pleasure of living. For this reason, confession is one of the most liberating kinds of prayer you will ever experience. The psalmist describes God's desire for our confession and cleansing when he says, "...A broken and contrite heart, O God, you will not despise." (Psalm 51:17b, NIV)

The Lord desires our prayers of confession because of our need, but such prayers would never have to be prayed if it were not for the problem of sin, so we need to answer the questions, "What is sin? And where does it come from?"

WHAT IS SIN?

In a broad sense, there are only two kinds of sin. The best-understood is the *sin of commission*. Paul defines this form in 1 John 3:4: "Sin is the transgression of the law." (1 John 3:6, KJV) This means willfully breaking the Ten Commandments or doing what you *know* to be wrong.

I vividly remember my first conscious decision to do this. I was just a little boy, but I understood exactly what I was doing. One warm summer afternoon I saw two glistening green Coke bottles which belonged to the Johnsons, our next-door neighbors. For some reason, the bottles looked as appealing to me as emeralds would to an adult. A very real battle took place within my mind. It was as if Satan and God were each stating their case. I knew inwardly it was wrong to steal. For what seemed an eternity, I paced up and down the driveway separating our houses. Then I willfully chose to become a thief and ran to get the Coke bottles as fast as I could.

As soon as I crossed the driveway and headed home, the full impact of my decision struck me. Suddenly the bottles in my hands lost all their glamor. I can distinctly recall a feeling I had never experienced before. It was as if something wonderful had died! Immediately I told God I was sorry and took the Coke bottles back, placing them behind the bush by the porch where I had found them. That painful experience was followed by other willful, sinful decisions which finally led me to admit my need of a Savior.

The other category of sin is described by James, "Knowing what is right to do and then not doing it is sin." (James 4:17, NIV) This is generally called the *sin of omission*.

God expressed his disdain for this kind of sin when He asked, "Will a man rob God? Yet you rob Me. But you ask, 'How do we rob You?' In tithes and offerings . . . Bring the whole tithe into the storehouse, that there may be food in My house. 'Test Me in this,' says the Lord Almighty, 'and see if I will not throw open the floodgates of heaven and pour out so much blessing that you will not have room enough for it.'" (Malachi 3:8 & 10, NIV)

The omission of giving 10 percent of your income back to the Lord is as sinful as embezzling an extra 10 percent from the business where you work. Once you understand this, you will see why so much is said in the Bible about the importance of stewardship. Giving is not only a command, but a tangible expression of our love. Jesus said, "If you love Me, keep My commandments." (John 14:15, NKJV)

The sin of omission reflects an irresponsible attitude, and the Bible says, "Do not withhold good from those who deserve it, when it is in your power to act." (Proverbs 3:27, NIV) It is always a Christian's responsibility to do what is right.

The overall teaching of the Bible, with regard to sin, is best summarized in the words of Paul, who said, "Whatsoever is not of faith is sin." (Romans 14:23v, KJV) What does this mean? If on the basis of God's Word you question the validity of an act, but you do it anyway, you are not acting in faith. On the contrary, you are acting out of doubt. This means you are proceeding on your own without praying and waiting for God's clear leading.

A tragic decision in the life of King Saul vividly demonstrates the meaning of this verse. He was told to go to a certain place and wait seven days for the prophet Samuel, who would prepare a special offering to sacrifice to the Lord (1 Samuel 10:8). But when Saul saw that the crowd gathered for the worship service was beginning to scatter, he became uncertain of what to do and took matters into his own hands. In direct disobedience to God's instruction, he personally offered the sacrifice which the prophet Samuel was to have made. Had Saul responded in faith rather than fear, he would have obeyed God in spite of the outward circumstances. His vacillating obedience brought forth a strong rebuke from God and caused him to lose his position of leadership.

This is an extreme example, but it underscores two important principles. First, when God gives you something to do, the outward circumstances will not always make it convenient to obey. When Jesus redeemed us, He experienced adversity and pain, but by faith He was obedient, even to the point of dying on a cross. If He had chosen the easy road rather than the path of faith, He would have failed in His divine mission. The same is true for us.

Second, a high percentage of life's mistakes are brought about by impatience. If Saul had asked the Lord for guidance and taken time to pray, how different his life would have been. It is important to remember that God is more interested in showing us His will than we are in finding it. If He says "go," go in faith! If He says "stop," stop in faith! If He doesn't say, wait in faith!

Paul said, "The righteous will live by faith." (Galatians 3:11, NIV) When we seek to do that, we are protected from sins of commission and omission.

WHERE DOES SIN COME FROM?

Above anything else, it must be said that sin does not come from God. The Bible says, "Let no one say when he is tempted, 'I am being tempted by God;' for God cannot be tempted by evil, and He Himself does not tempt anyone. But each one is tempted when he is carried away and enticed by his own lust. Then when lust has conceived, it gives birth to sin." (James 1:13-15)

When James says we are enticed by our *own lusts*, he is talking about the fallen nature of man. Since the earliest times, man has had an independent and often rebellious spirit. This is why Paul says, "for all have sinned and fall short of the glory of God." (Romans 3:23)

As a guest preacher in a small Western town, a close friend of mine was invited to stay in a private home. When morning came, he ate breakfast with a boy named Johnny, who was considered the "terror" of the neighborhood. As they ate, while his mother's back was turned, the boy picked up his bowl of cereal and milk and threw it upside down on the table. Much of it landed on my friend's good suit. Trying to comfort the mother in a very awkward situation, he said, "It's all right. That could have happened to anyone. I'll put on my other suit and be right back." When he returned, he looked at the little boy as if to say, "You wouldn't!"

But as soon as the mother turned her back, Johnny did it again! The mother was so unnerved she began to cry. Can you imagine hosting a visiting minister and having your child throw milk and cereal on him—twice? Realizing it wasn't an accident, the mother walked over to the table and asked, "Johnny, why did you do that?" Defiantly, the little boy looked up and said, "Mother, *I do as I please!*"

Down through the ages, man has glared at God in defiance saying, "I will do whatever I please." The Scripture says, "The heart is deceitful above all things, and desperately wicked." (Jeremiah 17:9a, KJV) It is the source of our self-will! Though he didn't know it, when little Johnny expressed his selfish feelings, they were coming from his heart. Jesus expressed this truth when He said, "For out of the abundance of the heart the mouth speaks." (Matthew 12:34b, NKJV)

In the final analysis, all sin is the result of the *self-will* which resides in the human heart. This is why no lasting change can take place in your life until Christ is enthroned as Lord in that domain!

Turning over a new leaf is inadequate in dealing with sin. Why? Because our outward acts are only symptoms of the deeper problem within. The Bible says, "For out of the heart come evil thoughts, murder, adultery, sexual immorality, theft, false testimony, and slander." (Matthew 15:19, NIV) This is why David cried out to God in confession after his tragic sin with Bathsheba, saying, "Create in me a clean heart, O God; and renew a right spirit within me." (Psalm 51:10, KJV) He knew the source of his sin.

Jesus enlarged on this truth when He explained that, "But I tell you that anyone who looks at a woman lustfully has already committed adultery with her in his heart." (Matthew 5:28, NIV) This is why the Bible says, "Keep your heart with all diligence, for out of it spring the issues of life." (Proverbs 4:23, NKJV)

CONFESSION AND REPENTANCE

Confession is admitting that you have chosen to do your will rather than God's. Repentance involves trusting God to change your heart as you willfully choose not to sin again.

Jesus' contemporary and cousin, John the Baptist, preached this message with biting practicality. When previously hypocritical religious leaders came to be baptized, he warned them to "bring forth fruit in keeping with repentance." (Matthew 3:8)

What did he mean by this? Sorrow or even verbal admission of our sin is not enough. Although God stands ready and willing to forgive us when we confess, He also requires changed actions, new priorities, and growth in our character. When Jesus forgave, He said, "...go and sin no more." (John 8:11b, KJV)

One evening as we talked in a coffee shop, a friend who was a new Christian asked for some advice about a matter of deep concern. His business partner of seven years had just voluntarily admitted embezzling a large sum of money from their jointly owned company. He was shocked almost beyond belief that his partner had betrayed his trust. Now he was thinking through his alternatives. Should he send the man to the penitentiary or let him go free and try to absorb the loss?

I could see that my friend deeply cared about his unconverted partner and wanted to do whatever was right in terms of the Scriptures. His partner was sorry for what he had done and had voluntarily confessed the crime. What more could he do? The Bible teaches that true confession is always accompanied by repentance. In this case, the evidence of real confession and repentance would be the willingness to repay the stolen money. After our discussion, my friend decided to ask his partner to sign a legally binding note, as if he had *borrowed* rather than stolen, the money. This would provide him an opportunity to prove his repentance.

To shed light on his own responsibility in the problem, my friend and I discussed the Scriptural injunctions which say, "Do not be yoked together with unbelievers." (2 Corinthians 6:14a, NIV), and, "What does a believer have in common with an unbeliever?" (2 Corinthians 6:15b, NIV) Having never read these verses before, he was shocked to learn that he had violated a very practical biblical principle and was partially responsible for the problem that had developed as a result.

WHY CONFESSION WORKS

A check is of no more value than the bank on which it is written, and forgiveness is available only because the grace of God is adequate to make it possible. If God were spiritually insolvent, confession would be a waste of time. However, the Scripture declares, "God shall supply all your needs according to His riches in glory in Christ Jesus." (Philippians 4:19) When we come to the Father in the name of His Son and our Savior, no matter how big our need might be, we have been assured that His boundless riches are there to make good our request.

How does this work? How can you, on earth, confess a sin in prayer and be assured of God's forgiveness in heaven? Paul explained the answer to that question in his letter to the believers at Corinth: "He (God the Father) made Him (Christ the Son) who knew no sin to be sin on our behalf, that we might become the righteousness of God in Him." (2 Corinthians 5:21) This miraculous exchange of guilt, in which Christ bore the full penalty of our sin, is the sole reason confession works. When we confess our sins, we are agreeing with God in two important respects: First, that what we did was not for His glory and was wrong; second, that His grace and power are fully adequate to provide the forgiveness we need.

If Jesus had not been sinless, He could not have been our Savior. One bankrupt person cannot borrow money from another. Describing all mankind, the Bible says, "There is none righteous, not even one." (Romans 3:10) Speaking of Christ's uniqueness, the Scripture depicts His sinless sacrifice using the illustration of a priest: "For it was fitting that we should have such a high priest, holy, innocent, undefiled, separated from sinners and exalted above the heavens, who does not need...to offer up sacrifices, first for His own sins, and then for the sins of the people, because this He did once for all when He offered up Himself." (Hebrews 7:26-27)

Not only is Christ adequate because He is sinless, but because

He understands us: "For we do not have a high priest who cannot sympathize with our weaknesses, but one who has been tempted in all things as we are, yet without sin." (Hebrews 4:15)

He lived His life victoriously, winning every battle on our behalf. The salvation He achieved was effective not only for those who had sought God by faith in the past, but for all who would accept Him as their Savior in the future. He did what no prophet, priest, or king could ever do on man's behalf. Because of His sacrificial death and saving life, confession and its cleansing effect are backed up by all the power and riches of God Himself.

CONFESSION RESTORES FELLOWSHIP

Once while driving down the highway, minding my own business, I was suddenly hit in the head by a hard plastic pink elephant. I had done nothing to provoke it, but it happened anyway. As a result, my daughter and I had a long talk about the fact that there was no excuse for that kind of behavior. While still unrepentant, she received a good spanking. Once she experienced a little of the pain she had inflicted, she understood why hitting people was wrong. Almost immediately her attitude changed, and our fellowship was restored.

She was still my child, even though she had hit me in the head with her pink elephant, but our fellowship was clouded until things were straightened out. Sin does not alter our relationship with God, but it does diminish the quality of joy we experience as His child.

We were created for the purpose of fellowship, so when we fail to walk in harmony with God, we bring Him little pleasure. Unconfessed sin hinders our fellowship with Him, because it creates a barrier in our prayer life, and prayer is our means of spiritual communication. Understanding this fact, the psalmist said, "If I had cherished sin in my heart, the Lord would not have listened." (Psalm 66:18, NIV)

Your relationship with Christ is eternal; it is solid and stable. You love Him, and He loves you, but confession of sin is necessary in order to maintain the normal joy and quality of that relationship.

CONFESSING TO ONE ANOTHER

Having looked at the vertical aspects of confession between you and God, there is another dimension that needs to be considered. You are also told to "confess your sins one to another, and pray for one another." (James 5:16a) The spirit of this teaching was made clear by the Lord when He delivered His famous Sermon on the Mount. He said, "Therefore if you bring your gift to the altar, and there remember that your brother has something against you, leave your gift there before the altar, and go your way. First be reconciled to your brother, and then come and offer your gift." (Matthew 5:23-24, NKJV)

Confessing a bad attitude or asking forgiveness for an act committed against your brother is even more important to God than your prayer of confession. Why is this true? Because character development and honesty are more important to God than mere words. He is constantly looking for change as the evidence of your spiritual growth.

> When you have your Quiet Time, be specific in relating every prayer of confession to a tangible change which you want to see in your life. Relate that change to the sin you are confessing.
>
> Never confess with the secret intent of committing that sin again. Always plan for spiritual improvement, and God will honor your faith with the strength to say "no" to temptation and "yes" to righteousness. Paul said, "I can do all things through Christ who strengthens me." (Philippians 4:13, NKJV)

CHAPTER 7

SHARING GOD'S PLAN OF SALVATION

No words can adequately describe the price God chose to pay to make forgiveness possible. Spend a moment in meditation, considering the fact that God Himself died to assure your salvation. Ask the Father to let the depth of this amazing truth fill your heart. Ask Him to reemphasize in your mind His eternal love expressed in His Son. Focus your thoughts on the person of Christ. Notice His radiance, strength, and His giving, yet demanding love. He was like no other man who ever lived, and yet was clearly, in every respect, fully man.

To share God's plan of salvation is to share a person—a sinless, victorious, living person. His very name explains His divine mission: "and they shall call His name Immanuel, which translated means, 'God with us,'" "for in Him all the fulness of Deity dwells in bodily form." (Matthew 1:23; Colossians 2:9)

Jesus said, "I and the Father are one." (John 10:30); "He who has seen Me, has seen the Father." (John 14:9:6b); "No one has taken [my life] from Me, but I lay it down on My own initiative. I have authority to lay it down, and I have authority to take it up again." (John 10:18); "Destroy this temple, and in three days I will raise it up." (John 2:19); "I am the door; if anyone enters through Me, he shall be saved, and shall go in and out, and find pasture." (John 10:9); "I am the living bread that came down out of heaven; if any one eats of the bread, he shall live forever." (John 6:51a); "whoever drinks of the water that I shall give him shall never thirst; but the water that I shall give him shall become in him a well of water springing up to eternal life." (John 4:14)

Of Him the Scriptures say; "He is the image of the invisible God, the first-born of all creation." (Colossians 1:15); "All things came into being through Him; and apart from Him nothing came into being." (John 1:3); "both in the heavens and on earth, visible and invisible, whether thrones or dominions or rulers or authorities—all things have been created through Him and for Him...and in Him all things hold together." (Colossians 1:16b-17); "He was in the world, and the world was made through Him, but the world did not know Him. He came to His own, and those who were His own did not receive Him. But as many as received Him, to them He gave the right to become children of God, even to those who believe in His name." (John 1:10-12)

Christ is man's single source of salvation. Not good works. Not world religious leaders. Not even religion itself. It is, simply and finally, Christ alone. Peter explained this to a large crowd after a lame man's ankles and feet were healed and strengthened in the powerful name of Jesus Christ. "There is salvation in no one else; for there is no other name under heaven that has been given among men, by which we must be saved." (Acts 4:12) Christ was the Father's single and all-sufficient plan for salvation. "For it was the Father's good pleasure for all the fulness to dwell in Him, and through Him to reconcile all things to Himself." (Colossians 1:19 & 20a)

As you share a word of truth and give your personal testimony, you also need to be able to present God's plan of salvation in a systematic fashion. You must be able to guide someone through the Scriptures so they can understand how to become a Christian.

FAITH PRODUCES BOLDNESS

I have always liked the story about the two men in a foxhole. They were totally surrounded by the enemy. John said, "Sam, we're completely surrounded by the enemy; they're everywhere."

Sam replied, "Good! Let's not let a single one get away!"

That's the kind of faith and aggressive spirit we need in evangelism. We are surrounded by a sea of need. People everywhere are hungry for Jesus Christ and for salvation, but many of them do not know what label to put on that hunger. They're searching for God, but often don't know who or what they are looking for.

Sharing a word of truth gives you an open door to find out a person's level of interest in spiritual things. Your *personal testimony* reveals the reality of Christ in your own experience. The *plan of salvation* indicates the simple but profound decision involved in receiving the gift of forgiveness and eternal life.

Philip explained salvation to a complete stranger during the earliest days of the church: "Now an angel of the Lord said to Philip, 'Go south to the road—the desert road—that goes down from Jerusalem to Gaza.' So he started out, and on his way he met an Ethiopian eunuch, an important official in charge of all the treasury of Candace, queen of the Ethiopians. This man had gone to Jerusalem to worship, and on his way home was sitting in his chariot reading the book of Isaiah the prophet. The Spirit told Philip, 'Go to that chariot and stay near it!'"

"Then Philip ran up to the chariot and heard the man reading Isaiah the prophet. 'Do you understand what you are reading?' Philip asked."

"'How can I,' he said, 'unless someone explains it to me?' So he invited Philip to come up and sit with him." (Acts 8:26-31)

The eunuch did not need a brief general witness about the goodness of God, nor did he need to hear Philip's testimony. What he wanted was a clear understanding of the Christ of Isaiah 53 and the knowledge of how to meet Him as his own Savior. Philip was both available and prepared, and the result was one of the significant conversions of the early church.

KNOWING HIM PERSONALLY

Jesus Christ is not only concerned with getting people interested in Him; He wants them to know Him personally. He wants to redeem them, and He wants them to have a definite conversion experience. This means you have to know how to lead others to an intelligent, forthright decision.

A person doesn't just ooze into Christ. There has to be a moment when he or she says, "Yes, I receive You as my own Lord and Savior."

A person must know that he or she is a Christian and not guess so, hope so, or think so. One of the ways you can help people have this settled assurance is through what has been called the Bridge Illustration. I frequently ask one of these two questions:

(1)   Do you think about spiritual things often?

(2)   Through the years have you come to know Christ personally, or are you still on the way?

This approach gently opens the door for explaining the Bridge Illustration.

THE BRIDGE ILLUSTRATION

Let's assume you are talking with someone who is interested and eager to listen. Get a sheet of paper (even a napkin will do) and write on it: "MAN" and "GOD" (Fig. 1). Explain that "Man has always wanted to know God and in a variety of ways has sought to worship Him."

Share the fact that a serious problem keeps us from having the quality relationship with God that we need and that He wants us to have. The Bible tells us about that problem in Romans 3:23—"For

MAN   GOD

Fig. 1

all have sinned and fall short of the glory of God."

Hand the person a Bible, point to that verse, and ask him to read it aloud to you. People do not want to hear your opinion about Jesus Christ. They want to see what the Bible says. The average person has a profound respect for the Bible, even though he may never have read it. Let the Scripture speak for itself.

After he has read the verse, carry on a conversation something like this: "Now, William, that verse you have just read says all have sinned. What does it say about you? Are you part of that *all?*"

"Yeah, I'm part of that all."

"Well, what does it say about you?"

"It says that I've sinned."

If he inquires about the rest of the verse, say, "William, 'Fallen short of the glory of God' means living a life that is imperfect. All of us have lived lives that are sinful and unlike that of Jesus Christ. His life was sinless and perfect, and all the world has fallen short of that standard."

It has been the author's experience that no one seems to feel his life measures up to that of Jesus. Therefore, they understand the concept of sin once this comparison has been made.

Write the reference "Romans 3:23" under "MAN," and write *"ALL HAVE SINNED"* next to it. Then draw the chasm between "MAN" and "GOD" and write "SIN" in that space (Fig. 2).

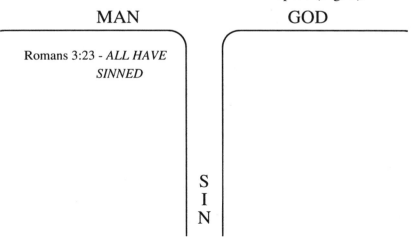

Fig. 2

Now turn to Romans 6:23 and have him read the verse aloud. "For the wages of sin is death, but the free gift of God is eternal life in Christ Jesus our Lord." The word "wages" needs some explanation. I usually say something like this: "William, have you ever worked for wages?"

He replies, "Yes, I have a job."

"All right, what is a wage?"

"It's the salary you earn. It's what you get on payday."

"The Bible says that sin earns death. When payday comes, death is what you will have earned. When a man sins and is separated from God, he is dead toward God and has no relationship with his Creator. So all have sinned, and because of your sin, you have earned spiritual death."

"William, two kinds of death are explained in the Bible. One is physical, which we're going to look at in a moment, and the other is spiritual, which the Bible is talking about here."

At this point pause to write down "Romans 6:23" in your illustration and the words, *"SIN EARNS SPIRITUAL DEATH"* next to it (Fig. 3).

Next, turn to Hebrews 9:27 and let him read aloud—"It is appointed for men to die once, and after this comes judgment."

Say, "This verse speaks of physical death. God has appointed a

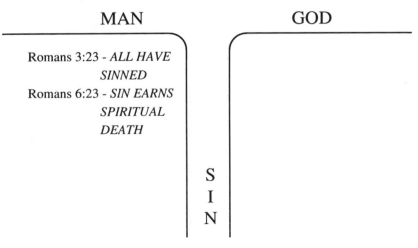

MAN   GOD

Romans 3:23 - *ALL HAVE SINNED*
Romans 6:23 - *SIN EARNS SPIRITUAL DEATH*

S
I
N

Fig. 3

time when every man, woman, boy and girl will die physically. Our brief time here on earth is to prepare for that all-important day. Only God knows when it will come.

"William, someday you're going to die, and so will I. After that we will face God's judgment. When we look at the facts, mankind has a real problem that adds up to eternal death."

Now write "Hebrews 9:27" under the other verses with the notation *"ALL DIE PHYSICALLY"* by it. Then summarize the results of these three verses in the words *"ETERNAL DEATH"* (Fig. 4). At this point you have clearly demonstrated William's condition.

Now you will be able to help him see the wonderful plan made possible by Christ's love. Begin with Romans 5:8—"But God demonstrates His own love for us in this: While we were still sinners, Christ died for us." (NIV) Emphasize the fact that God took the initiative while we were still guilty of our sin."

"William, you are in the midst of your sin, but God loves you just as you are."

On the right side of your illustration under "GOD" write "Romans 5:8" and by it the words *"CHRIST DIED FOR US WHILE WE WERE STILL SINNERS."* Then draw a cross, bridging the gap between "GOD" and "MAN" (Fig. 5). This is why Jesus went to the cross: to pay the penalty of our sin, so mark through the word "sin."

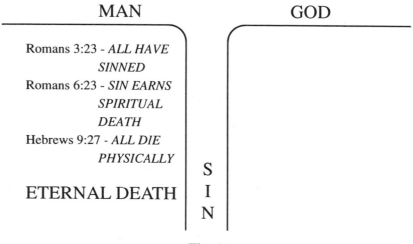

Fig. 4

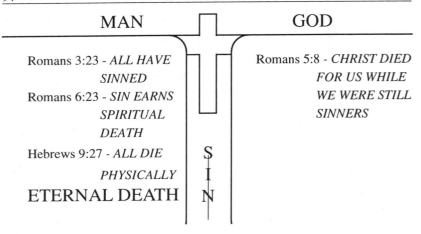

MAN	GOD
Romans 3:23 - *ALL HAVE SINNED* Romans 6:23 - *SIN EARNS SPIRITUAL DEATH* Hebrews 9:27 - *ALL DIE PHYSICALLY* **ETERNAL DEATH**	Romans 5:8 - *CHRIST DIED FOR US WHILE WE WERE STILL SINNERS*

Then turn to Ephesians 2:8 & 9—"For it is by grace you have been saved, through faith—and this not from yourselves, it is the gift of God—not by works, so that no one can boast." (NIV)

"William, it is by God's grace and love that we are able to become Christians. It is love you don't deserve and a love you can never earn. If a gift is offered that must be earned, it isn't a gift. And salvation is something God gives us because He loves us. It is strictly a gift."

I once tested this with my secretary. I called her into my office and said, "If I were to give you your paycheck in a gift-wrapped box, what would be your immediate response?"

She answered, "Real disappointment. I would open the gift thinking it was a bonus—something extra special. Then I would discover it was only my paycheck. I would think, 'Are you hinting that I haven't been earning my wages? Why would you consider my paycheck a gift?'"

Explain to your inquirer that salvation is a gift from God, which cannot be received on the basis of merit.

Write "Ephesians 2:8 & 9" on the right side and by it the words *"BY GOD'S LOVE WE ARE SAVED THROUGH FAITH."* (Fig. 6).

Next turn to John 1:12 and ask your friend to read this verse to you – "Yet to all who received Him, to those who believed in His name, He gave the right to become children of God." (NIV) Pay close attention to the two key words—*believe* and *receive*.

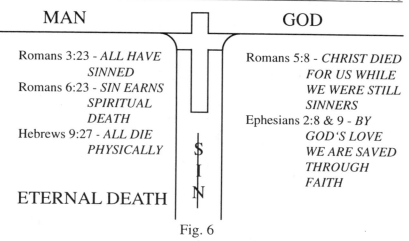

MAN	GOD
Romans 3:23 - *ALL HAVE SINNED* Romans 6:23 - *SIN EARNS SPIRITUAL DEATH* Hebrews 9:27 - *ALL DIE PHYSICALLY* ETERNAL DEATH	Romans 5:8 - *CHRIST DIED FOR US WHILE WE WERE STILL SINNERS* Ephesians 2:8 & 9 - *BY GOD'S LOVE WE ARE SAVED THROUGH FAITH*

Fig. 6

Now say, "William, there are two steps in this verse that explain how to become a child of God. The first is to believe in Jesus Christ. You must honestly accept that He is who He claimed to be. Do you believe that He was born of a virgin, that He lived a sinless life, that He died for your sins, and that He rose from the grave in victory? If you do, you will be eager to take the second step, which is to receive Him as your own Savior and Lord."

Ultimately, you are leading William to see that Jesus is God and that his decision about Jesus means accepting or rejecting God. Intellectual acceptance is not enough. The act of faith must occur for the rebirth to be experienced. William must exercise his will to receive Christ into his life.

At this point, draw a bridge across the top of the cross on your diagram and write "BELIEVE AND RECEIVE" and "John 1:12" over the top of the bridge; also write "ETERNAL LIFE" on the right side (Fig. 7).

To illustrate the difference between believing and receiving, take a pen or pencil and ask, "William, do you believe that I have a pen in my hand?"

"Yes, I do."

"Well, do you believe it enough that if I offer it to you, you will take it?" You offer it, and he takes it.

Now ask, "William, what did you just do?"

"I took it."

John 1:12

BELIEVE AND RECEIVE

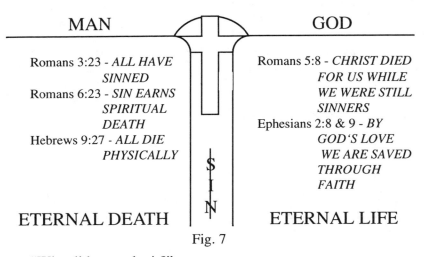

MAN	GOD
Romans 3:23 - *ALL HAVE SINNED* Romans 6:23 - *SIN EARNS SPIRITUAL DEATH* Hebrews 9:27 - *ALL DIE PHYSICALLY*	Romans 5:8 - *CHRIST DIED FOR US WHILE WE WERE STILL SINNERS* Ephesians 2:8 & 9 - *BY GOD'S LOVE WE ARE SAVED THROUGH FAITH*
ETERNAL DEATH	ETERNAL LIFE

Fig. 7

"Why did you take it?"

"Because you offered it to me."

"In other words, you believed me when I said I would give it to you, so you were willing to reach out to receive it."

He responds, "That's right."

"William, the pen was potentially yours the moment I decided to offer it, but it wasn't yours *experientially* until you acted in faith and *received* it.

"What Christ did on the cross was potentially for everyone in the world. The gift has already been paid for, and the loving hand of God is now extended. He is waiting for you and every other person to believe in Him and receive His gift that He offers in Christ."

(Because I am typically drawing the Bridge Illustration on a piece of paper with a pen or pencil, this is my favorite way to explain John 1:12).

UNUSUAL CIRCUMSTANCES

Under unusual circumstances, you may have to do something more dramatic to drive home the truth.

I was trying to get this point across one day in West Texas to a cowboy at a camp meeting.

I said to him, "Mr. Taylor, you can't receive Christ until you believe in Him."

"Oh, I've always believed in Him," he replied.

"Yes, but have you ever received Him? Has it ever gone beyond 'there is a God in heaven,' and 'Yes, Christ is the Son of God?'"

I showed him the Bridge Illustration, but I couldn't seem to get him to understand the nature of the decision he needed to make. He seemed to have a barrier in his mind. So I finally enacted a parable to express the truth about receiving Christ. I looked out across the camp toward his cabin and said, "Mr. Taylor, your cabin is on fire."

He took off immediately, running to put the fire out.

Soon he came back, saying, "Billie, why did you tell me my cabin was on fire? There wasn't any fire."

I said, "I wanted to illustrate the verse we were talking about— the one about believing and receiving."

"What do you mean?"

"Did you believe what I said about the fire?"

"Sure I believed you! I went to put the fire out."

"All right, Mr. Taylor, let me show you something. A few minutes ago you said you believed in the Lord Jesus Christ, yet you have refused to pray and receive Him as your Lord. True belief requires action. Mr. Taylor, the day you truly believe in Jesus Christ, you will have no option but to pray and receive Him as your Lord and your God. Until that time, you may admire Him, respect Him, and even fear Him, but according to the Bible, you do not really believe in Him until you receive Him."

DEALING WITH SELF-WORTH

In sharing the plan of salvation, you will discover that most people fall into one of two categories. One doesn't believe God is *adequate* to save them. The other doesn't believe they are *worth* saving. Many times it is helpful for them to see this difference themselves.

I first learned the importance of this fact while talking to a geologist who truly wanted to be saved. After we talked for some time, I finally said, "Let's assume I am with Exxon, and I have come to offer you a million-dollar retainer, because we feel you are such a brilliant geologist. I want you to be available to our geological staff. We don't want you to do any specific work, we just want you to be available for future consultation. On that basis, would you take the check?"

"You bet, I'd take it!"

"Do you think the check would bounce?"

"Of course not. That's why I would take it."

He believed in the financial strength of Exxon; therefore, he would gladly take the check.

I said, "Mr. Wright, do you believe that God is strong enough to forgive your sins?"

"I never thought about it like that." he replied. "I do believe that He's that powerful."

"All right, then, what you are saying is that you already have faith in Exxon and you want to have faith in God. Mr. Wright, there are only two reasons why an honest man would not take the Exxon retainer. The first would be that he didn't believe that Exxon was worth the money, and you have negated that. The second would be that you don't believe you are worth the amount of the retainer. Is that why you haven't received Jesus Christ?"

His look of surprise was followed by the dawn of understanding. It was deeply fulfilling to observe the change in his countenance as he realized that his feelings of low self-worth had been the elusive barrier that had hindered him in his desire to know God. After discussing Romans 5:8 again, warm tears were followed by an earnest decision to receive Christ.

Countless millions of people are outside the kingdom waiting to be assured that in God's eyes, they are *worth* saving.

Now return to your completed diagram (Fig. 7) and ask the person to whom you are witnessing: "William, where are you on this diagram? Are you on the left side (MAN) or are you on the right (GOD)? Or somewhere in between?"

When that question is asked, the average person will put his finger in the middle, on the "AND" between "BELIEVE" and "RECEIVE." He has not understood how to commit himself. He will often say, "Yes, I believe in Christ, but no, I've never personally received Him as my Savior."

Many good, moral people have an intellectual belief in Christ but have never committed themselves to receiving Him. Actually, when they put their finger on the "AND" in the middle, they have helped you recognize exactly where they are.

You can now say to the person, "Wonderful! William, you've taken the first step; you already believe in Christ. Now wouldn't you like to finish it? Wouldn't you like to take the next step and actually receive Him into your life?"

The usual answer is, "Yes, I would. No one's ever explained how before."

The next step is a prayer, which I call the Sinner's Prayer.

THE SINNER'S PRAYER

After a person has seen his need of conversion, it is a dangerous thing to leave him without help in the area of prayer. Over the years, I have learned there is much value in memorizing the seven basic elements to a sinner's prayer. Learn these, so that when God gives you someone who is ready to receive Him, you will be prepared.

The seven ingredients are confession, contrition, repentance, invitation, consecration, dependence, and thanksgiving. (You will find the first five of these elements in the Parable of the Prodigal Son—Luke 15:11-32, particularly verses 17-21).

The words for each section are:

1. Confession—"Lord Jesus, I am a sinner."
2. Contrition—"But I am sorry for my sins."
3. Repentance—"I want to turn from my sins; I am willing to begin a new life with Your help."
4. Invitation—"Lord Jesus, please come into my heart and life right now."

5. Consecration—"From this moment forward, my life belongs to You and You alone."

6. Dependence—"I will love You, serve You, and tell others about You, and trust You to live Your life through me."

7. Thanksgiving—"Thank You, Lord, for coming into my life and for forgiving my sins today."

After you pray a prayer like that with a person, the next thing you should do is show them 1 John 5:11-13 – "And this is the testimony: God has given us eternal life, and this life is in His Son. He who has the Son has life; he who does not have the Son of God does not have life. I write these things to you who believe in the name of the Son of God so that you may *know* that you have eternal life." (NIV)

This lets the new believer know what the Bible says about the assurance they can have regarding their decision to receive Christ.

For some who are reading this book, this might be the most important section as you consider your own life. Come to a deep assurance concerning the promise of these verses. I have never met a powerful witness who did not have an equally solid conviction concerning their assurance of salvation in Christ.

Assurance is more than a feeling. It is an unshakable, eternal promise. "He who has the Son has life." If you do not have this assurance, read the sinner's prayer, slowly and thoughtfully. If you have never been sure in the past, let today seal this matter for eternity. Ask Christ into your heart, and begin to thank Him that from this moment forward you can know beyond question that you have eternal life.

CHAPTER 8

PETITION

A GREAT INVITATION

God has petitioned us to make petitions. He said, "Call to Me, and I will answer you, and I will tell you great and mighty things, which you do not know." (Jeremiah 33:3) This is an amazing invitation coupled with an equally amazing promise. Toward the end of Jesus' earthly ministry, He encouraged His disciples with these words: "Until now you have asked for nothing in My name; ask, and you will receive, that your joy may be made full." (John 16:24)

Because of God's love and the disciples' belief that Jesus had come "forth from the Father," (John 16:27) a wonderful *change* in their prayer life was about to take place. This would occur when they would see Him again after His crucifixion and resurrection (John 16:17b, 25). At that time, He would no longer speak to them using parables and allegories but would teach them in simplest words about the Father and His kingdom. By then, they would be ready to better understand the deep truths He wanted to communicate.

PRAYING IN THE NAME OF JESUS CHRIST

After His resurrection, there would be no further need for Jesus to humanly make requests of the Father on their behalf. Those who believed in Him would be able to go directly to the Father offering their petitions in His name (John 16:26).

This was a new teaching. For centuries, Hebrew believers had prayed to Jehovah God based upon their faith, and that faith had been demonstrated by their obedience in offering sacrifices at the Temple in Jerusalem. But now, the Father was providing the *timeless* and *sinless* sacrifice of His only begotten Son, the Lamb of God. From this time forward, all who entered into the forgiveness and cleansing made possible through that sacrifice could go directly to the Father in prayer. How? "In Jesus' name." Why? Because salvation through faith in Christ would open wide the everlasting door of personal *access to* and *fellowship with* God.

Through that perfect sacrifice, the wall of sin separating man and God would at last be removed! The Bible says, "There is no other name under heaven that has been given among men, by which we must be saved." (Acts 4:12) Through faith in Christ, we may now "come boldly unto the throne of grace." (Hebrews 4:16a, KJV) All of this and much more was made possible when the Lord ended the Old Testament sacrificial system by giving "His life as a ransom for many." (Matthew 20:28b) No saint, prophet, or priest in history could have done it, because the life of the Savior had to be *perfect* and *sinless*—as the Bible declares, a "lamb without blemish." (1 Peter 1:18 & 19, KJV)

Your prayers sit solidly upon the foundation of Jesus Christ's sinless life, sacrificial death, and victorious resurrection. That is why prayer in His name works!

UNDERSTANDING THE LORD'S PROMISE

Perhaps it startled the Lord's disciples when He said, "If you ask *anything* in My name, I will do it." (John 14:14, NKJV) It sounded as if He were giving them a license to ask for anything they might happen to want. However, some important *prerequisites* were provided for their protection and ours.

Prayer is not like giving a loaded gun to a child. God is fully aware of both our circumstances and the true motives behind our petitions. Referring to the barren results of prayerlessness, the Bible says, "You have not because you ask not." (James 4:2c) But it also says, "You ask and do not receive, because you ask with wrong motives." (James 4:3a)

Jesus' early disciples felt the need to pray, so they asked Him to teach them how (Luke 11). Later, when He related their prayers of petition to the fact that the Father would soon be sending the Holy Spirit to indwell them, He said, "He will teach you all things, and bring to your remembrance all that I said to you." (John 14:26) Against the background of that promise, Jesus did not hesitate to say, "And whatever you ask in My name, that will I do, that the Father may be glorified in the Son." (John 14:13)

If their prayers were based upon the wise instruction of the indwelling Holy Spirit and Jesus' earthly teachings, then their petitions would be the kind God would want to grant. Their prayers would bring glory to the Father.

FIRST PREREQUISITE

Jesus said, "If you abide in Me, and My words abide in you, ask whatever you wish, and it shall be done for you." (John 15:7)

Although the Bible teaches that everyone in the world was created by Christ, the word "if" in this verse makes it clear that abiding in Him is a *choice*. Abiding is descriptive of salvation. The way the Lord used the term, two complementary thoughts are combined—*resting in* because you are a *part of*.

To better understand His use of the word "abide," consider a tree. A limb rests in the trunk because it is an integral part of the tree. A Christian rests or abides in Christ because of the spiritual unity which has taken place in the experience of conversion, or what the Bible describes as being "born again" (John 3:3). Abiding or resting in salvation is the first prerequisite for answered prayers of petition.

SECOND PREREQUISITE

The second prerequisite has to do with Scripture. The Lord said if "My words abide in you." Before you can know how to accomplish His will, you need the guidance of His Word enabling you to pray with understanding. Allowing the Lord's words to abide in you means they are truly at home in your mind, because they have become a part of you.

Jeremiah expressed it this way: "Thy words were found, and I did eat them; and Thy word was unto me the joy and rejoicing of mine heart." (Jeremiah 15:16, KJV) He internalized God's word, and it literally became a part of him.

For this to happen to us, Bible study and Scripture memorization are essential. As we internalize the Scriptures, we come to understand how to pray *according to His will*. The Bible says, "And this is the confidence which we have before Him, that if we ask anything according to His will, He hears us. And...we know that we have the requests which we have asked from Him." (1 John 5:14 & 15)

Never once were the Lord Jesus' requests denied. Why? Because He prayed according to the Scriptures and always wanted His Father's will (Luke 22:42b). He didn't question it, doubt it, or rebel against it—He did it. This was the key to His unparalleled power in prayer.

THIRD PREREQUISITE

A third prerequisite has to do with the attitude of your heart. The Bible says, "Delight yourself also in the Lord; and He will give you the desires of your heart." (Psalm 37:4)

Not all of your prayers will be verbalized. Some will remain in the quiet recesses of your thoughts; however, both your spoken and unspoken prayers are important to God. The psalmist said, "Let the *words* of my mouth and the *meditation* of my heart be acceptable in Thy sight, O Lord, my rock and my redeemer." (Psalm 19:14)

Because God looks upon your heart, He knows exactly what you desire (1 Chronicles 28:9b). Your petitions never escape His notice, and He knows the motivations from which they spring. When He is your delight and His kingdom is what you are seeking, He can trust you with many privileges you would otherwise be unable to enjoy. The Bible says, "No good thing does He (the Lord) withhold from those who walk uprightly." (Psalm 84:11b)

Your petitions will be denied, however, if your desires are improper. James says, "You ask and do not receive because you ask with the wrong motives." (James 4:3)

WHY GOD SOMETIMES SAYS "NO"

Prayers of petition are exciting because of our sense of expectancy; but there are many occasions when we can thank God that our requests are answered with a "no" rather than a "yes."

At the low water mark in Moses' life, he said, "I cannot carry all these people by myself; the burden is too heavy for me." (Numbers 11:14, NIV) He had unconsciously shifted the weight of ministry off God's lofty shoulders onto his own. The result was depression, which led to this strange prayer of petition: "If I have found favor in Thy sight, please kill me at once." (Numbers 11:15b)

In this unusual petition, Moses presumed to understand his own problem and the best possible solution. It never occurred to him to turn the situation over to God and simply ask Him to take care of it. However, because He fully understood Moses' circumstances, He solved the problem rather than granting his request.

Moses' feelings of inadequacy and frustration were gently lifted when he received an unexpected answer. He was told to share his leadership responsibilities with seventy godly men. The Lord said, "They will help you carry the burden of the people so that you will not have to carry it alone." (Numbers 11:17b, NIV) God said "no" to Moses' request because of the unfulfilled potential of his life. He did not need to die. He did need to delegate.

How fortunate it is that in God's wisdom our petitions are not always granted. He loves us. He not only listens to our words but responds to the actual need behind our prayers.

WHEN YOU DON'T KNOW HOW TO PRAY

A fable is told about two monks who lived in a monastery hidden high in the mountains. Each was given the responsibility of caring for a seedling pine tree. They decided to compare the growth of their trees one year from the day when they were planted.

When that date finally arrived, one tree had died, while the other was hearty and beautiful. The disheartened monk with the lifeless tree came to discuss the matter with his colleague, producing a long list of dated petitions he had offered for his tree. The list included sunshine on some days, rain on others, and protection from insects and specific diseases. He had even asked for wind, frost, and snow to strengthen the little tree's endurance.

Curious to know what he had done wrong, he was eager to see the other monk's list. To his surprise, he had none! His daily petition had been a simple prayer in which he said, "Lord, You know that I am unsuited for the responsibility of caring for this little tree. But You also know its every need, because You created it. So please make it grow for Your glory."

The moral to this story is worth remembering: When in doubt about how to pray, pray anyway and trust your need to God, allowing *Him* to determine the answer. There is no circumstance beyond His knowledge, and there is no need too small or too large for His care.

The Bible says, "Do not be anxious about anything, but in everything, by prayer and petition, with thanksgiving, present your requests to God." (Philippians 4:6, NIV)

A "NO" FROM GOD MEANS A "YES" TO SOMETHING BETTER

I drive a Chevrolet Suburban, but my heart has always belonged to sports cars. You can imagine my thrill when my parents and grandmother called my university dorm years ago to say they had bought me a beautiful used gold Corvette. It had the biggest engine available and a four-speed transmission that almost caused the car to jump in first and second gears.

As soon as I hung up the phone, I felt impelled to pray. I petitioned, "Father, I'm so grateful for this car, but I just want to double-check whether or not You really want me to have it." I had never consciously prayed for a Corvette, but God knew how badly I had wanted one!

A question came to mind as I offered my prayer for guidance: "Do you love your Sunday school class?" And I answered, "I sure do." My class of corner newspaper salesmen and shoeshine boys was an informal but regular group of seven. I picked them up every Sunday morning in my Valiant station wagon. God spoke to my heart, "Billie, how do you think you are going to get all those kids in that little Corvette?"

"Well, I could take off the top and let them hang out!"

God made it very clear as I prayed that I must decide whether ministry to people or the love of things was going to be the overriding principle in my life. I was fearful of disappointing my parents and my grandmother, but to my surprise they gladly affirmed my decision. In fact, they allowed me to choose a new, more expensive Pontiac that had "four on the floor" and three two-barrel carburetors—but it was big enough to hold plenty of boys. Soon a caravan of three cars was required to handle the growth of the class!

God's "no" to the sports car was not a "no" to fun or beauty. It was simply His means of giving me a "yes" to something safer, better, and more usable at that stage of my life.

HOW TO PRAY IN THE HARD TIMES

Ultimately, in every person's experience there comes a time to ask the question, "How do I pray in this most difficult situation?" Recently I wrote a letter to a concerned husband who needed an answer to that question. His beloved wife was critically ill with cancer. What kind of petition should he bring to God in this circumstance?

A mature prayer would be: "Lord, I love the precious wife You have given me, and I thank You for being with her during this time of great need. I ask that You bring glory to Yourself through this difficult experience. If this can be accomplished by healing her, please do it, and I will thank You with all my heart. But if it will bring You greater glory to take her to Yourself, then please give me the strength to serve You and praise You when she is gone. I do not doubt Your love for her, nor Your power to heal her. Father, I know that our best interest is always on Your heart and that You will make no mistake in this matter. So whether she lives or whether she dies, let our witness be the kind that will bring others to faith in Christ."

Where is the mature faith in this prayer? It is found in these words: "I know that our best interest is always on Your heart and that You will make no mistake in this matter." Knowing that hard times would come, the Lord made this promise: "Fear not, for I am with you; be not dismayed, for I am your God. I will strengthen you. Yes, I will help you, I will uphold you with My righteous right hand." (Isaiah 41:10, NKJV)

The measure of maturity in one's petitions does not have to do with the size of the request—for with God nothing is impossible (Luke 1:37). He is not impressed by a loud voice, a tone of authority, or the scope of our petition. What pleases Him is the nature of our prayer. When we love Him enough to desire His glory more than deliverance from our temporary inconvenience or hardship, it brings Him great joy.

Nowhere is this more clearly demonstrated than in the prayers of Jesus. When He was agonizing in the Garden of Gethsemane and preparing for His most difficult hour, He said, "Father, if you are willing, take this cup from me: yet not my will, but yours be done." (Luke 22:42, NIV) Which would bring God the greater glory: for Jesus to be delivered from Calvary or for Him to go through Calvary? The adversity of the cross was the gateway to victory. Without the crucifixion, there could be no resurrection.

You will be most like Jesus when the preoccupation of your life is glorifying your heavenly Father. It was the Savior who prayed, "I have glorified you on the earth. I have finished the work which You have given Me to do." (John 17:4, NKJV)

THE PRINCIPLE OF VICTORY

Few men in history have understood as much about effective

prayer as the apostle Paul. The book of Acts is filled with "yes" answers to Paul's requests; however, in one notable instance God said, "No." Paul wrote the Christians in Corinth about his prayers concerning a physical infirmity which he described as a "thorn in the flesh." He said, "I entreated the Lord three times that it might depart from me, and He has said to me, 'My grace is sufficient for you, for My power is perfected in weakness.'" (2 Corinthians 12:8 & 9)

When Paul went to Galatia to preach the Gospel, it is clear that he arrived with a physical infirmity. At a later date, he reminded them of this fact, saying, "It was because of a bodily illness that I preached the gospel to you the first time; and that which was a trial to you in my bodily condition you did not despise or loathe...If possible, you would have plucked out your eyes and given them to me." (Galatians 4:13-15)

It is obvious that Paul's problem had continued, since he concluded his letter by saying, "See with what large letters I am writing to you." (Galatians 6:11) At that point, he took the pen from his secretary and wrote these words himself to prove the authenticity of the letter.

Although the great apostle had been the instrument through whom God had healed many others, in this instance it was not God's will for him to be healed. If Paul could heal himself or others *at will*, you can imagine the temptation toward pride. But if he had to leave Trophimus, his friend, sick at Miletus (2 Timothy 4:20b) and could not heal himself, he would constantly be reminded of his total dependence on God.

Because the Lord wanted to protect Paul from exalting himself, He intentionally left him with this infirmity (2 Corinthians 12:7b). Once Paul understood that God could work through him with greater spiritual power if he remained in physical weakness, the victory was won. He rejoiced saying, "Most gladly, therefore, I will rather boast about my weaknesses, that the power of Christ may dwell in me. . . for when I am weak, then I am strong." (2 Corinthians 12:9, 10b)

This principle was vividly illustrated again when Paul and Silas were harshly beaten with rods and placed in stocks in the Philippian jail. The two men sat there bleeding while singing and praising God. It was for God's glory that they remained in pain until after the doors were miraculously opened, and they went to their jailer's house. There the repentant Gentile jailer mercifully cleansed their backs and washed their wounds. Because of their testimony, an entire family was saved that night (Acts 16:22-34). It was through physical suffering that God was glorified.

Was that the kind of answer you expected or wanted the last time you offered a petition? Probably not! Our human nature recoils at the suggestion that suffering, pain, financial reverses, or the loss of something dear to us could be good.

It is only with maturity that we come to understand Paul's words that "all things work together for good to those who love God." (Romans 8:28, NKJV) If he had not experienced hunger, criticism, stonings, beatings, shipwrecks, imprisonment, and disappointment (2 Corinthians 6:4-6), perhaps those words would sound idealistic. But from his lips they are nothing less than a challenge for all Christians to live above their circumstances and experience inward victory.

WHEN GOD SAYS "YES"

Those who keep prayer lists have long since discovered that the overwhelming majority of their prayers are answered with a "yes." If the multitude of divine "yes" answers could be cataloged, it is doubtful that any computer ever made could contain them. From the first prayer ever prayed until now, the number would be staggering, because millions of God's children bring their small and large petitions to Him daily.

For the one time when God said "no" to Moses' request to take his life, there were scores of times when God positively answered his prayers for protection and guidance. En route to the promised land of Canaan, God's children received a constant succession of "yeses." With the slavery of Egypt behind them and the promise of milk, honey, and freedom ahead of them, they still faced all the obstacles which a barren wilderness affords.

As Moses sought God's direction, he said, "I pray, if I have found grace in Your sight, show me now Your way." (Exodus 33:13a, NKJV) God's immediate and comforting answer is typical of His response to our own petitions as we seek to do His will. He said, "My presence shall go with you, and I will give you rest." (Exodus 33:14) Moses wanted to know His way but received even more than he asked for. God not only wants to show us His way, but to personally walk with us in those blessed paths. Beyond that, He also promises rest on the journey.

Knowing how God feels about you as His child should be your greatest motivation for bringing Him your petitions in faith. He wants to say "yes," and your petitions are invited. What greater reason could you have for expressing your needs and desires to Him throughout the day.

As you bring your petitions to God, seeking His will, you can expect a "yes" but by faith must be equally willing to accept a "no." This quality of prayer is best achieved by spending time in the Scriptures and meditating upon what you read and hear. This will enable His words to "abide in you." Remember, you have been instructed to "let your requests be made known to God," (Philippians 4:6) with the promise that "the peace of God, which surpasses all understanding, will guard your hearts and minds through Christ Jesus." (Philippians 4:7, NKJV)

CHAPTER 9

GIVING IS WORSHIP

While researching the Biblical principles of giving, I considered the subject of worship. Frankly, I had never before studied worship in detail to find God's point of view. I have come to the conclusion that giving, along with our thanksgiving and praise, is worship.

In the past I made pledges to my church to be paid on a yearly basis. Once a month, I would write a check while in church and drop it in the collection plate. Sometimes I would mail a check from my office. My objective was for the church to get the total pledge before the end of the year. Though I had already experienced the joy of giving, the *act* of making my gift had little relationship to worship.

While I was writing this book, God convicted me to begin giving every time I went to church. The verse that spoke to me about this was Deuteronomy 16:16—"No man should appear before the Lord empty-handed." (NIV) When I started doing this, if a check were not handy, I gave cash. At first I thought about keeping up with the money given. Then God convicted me again. He seemed to say, "You do not need to keep up with the amount of cash. Give to Me simply out of a heart of love, and see how much you enjoy the service." I made this change in giving habits, and it has greatly enhanced my joy in our worship services.

WE WORSHIP WHAT WE LOVE

Many of us know by heart what Jesus called the greatest commandment: "Thou shalt love the Lord thy God with all they heart." But we know little about expressing this love through giving. In the writings of Moses we are told that the Lord drew His people to Himself at a special place of worship. Though the distances were great and many had to walk, still they came to express their devotion to God. Continually He sought to build their faith and deepen their character by teaching them how to express their love.

For this reason, Scripture says, "Every man shall give as he is able, according to the blessing of the Lord thy God which he hath given thee." (Deuteronomy 16:17, KJV) This passage reveals two important principles: First, God is leading e*veryone* to give. And second, we are to give as we have been blessed. This same principle is taught by the apostle Paul in 1 Corinthians 16:2—"Upon the first day of the week let every one of you lay by him in store, as God hath prospered him."

In Deuteronomy 16:10 & 11, we find an additional emphasis: "Then you shall celebrate...with...a freewill offering of your hand, which you shall give just as the Lord your God blesses you; and you shall rejoice before the Lord your God." This gift was to be over and above the tithe which had already been reserved by God out of the "first fruits." Why this additional instruction on giving?

Man's heart is so constructed that he will worship what he *really* loves. We worship what we love—we love what we worship. Inevitably, a man will spend time and money on that which he loves deeply. In Deuteronomy 16:17 the expression *"give as he is able"* does not refer only to giving in proportion to one's earnings. As a matter of practice, most people do give in proportion to what they earn. But the words "as he is able" also relate to a man's spirituality. Ultimately, we give as we are *enabled* by our spiritual growth and maturity. We have trouble giving when it is not done on the basis of faith and obedience. For example, if the Lord tells us to make a specific gift separate and apart from our tithe, we may react by saying, "Lord, I can't do that." This statement is exactly right. *We* can't do it—but He can: Our sufficiency is not of self, but of God (2

Corinthians 3:5).

It is important that we give as God directs, and not simply impulsively or out of fleshly motives. I have a good friend of long standing who was both aggressive as a businessman and abounding in spiritual activities. He actually neglected his business to "serve the Lord." We were both part of a group of businessmen who worked as a team in Christian service.

Every time this group wanted someone to go witnessing, to speak at meetings, or to join us in giving money to needy Christian causes, he was always in on the project on the same basis as the rest of us. The problem, as we found out later, was that he was giving out of his own resources—and he simply did not have enough resources. His excesses finally caught up with him when his business failed. He was so anxious to serve the Lord "like the others," and always to be in on the action, that he would "overcommit." He "over-served" out of enthusiasm before he had truly learned how to understand God's leading. He overextended himself in time as well as money.

This man finally removed himself from business and went full-time into the ministry. When his business books were closed, he owed about forty thousand dollars. I am happy to report that at the end of seven years, God so convicted him of his unpaid debts that he went back into business and in five years paid off his entire debt. Today this man has a good balance between business and ministry. He is one of the most effective Christian businessmen I know.

Warning: Do not overcommit your time or money. God never gets in a hurry. In the gospels I never see Jesus running, but always see Him walking. God has perfect timing for all of us. I know from experience how easy it is to get priorities rearranged in order to satisfy my ego and become a "people-pleaser."

Spirit-led giving leads us into a new dimension of joy because we are amazed to see God use us far beyond our expectations. When Scripture says, "I can do all things through Him who strengthens me," (Philippians 4:13) this includes spiritual giving as well.

WHAT GIFTS PLEASE GOD?

God is not impressed by the *size* of our gifts, but He is pleased by what we give out of specific obedience. This demonstrates our love for Him. The widow's example speaks volumes about a gift that pleases God:

> And He sat down opposite the treasury, and began observing how the multitude were putting money into the treasury; and many rich people were putting in large sums. And a poor widow came and put in two small copper coins, which amount to a cent. And calling His disciples to Him, He said to them, "Truly I say to you, this poor widow put in more than all the contributors to the treasury; for they all put in out of their surplus, but she, out of her poverty, put in all she owned, all she had to live on." (Mark 12:41-44)

An analysis of this passage reveals several interesting insights:
1. When you give to the Lord, He watches you with interest, just as He did in the case of this widow.
2. When you give, your gift can be a positive example to others. Jesus wanted His disciples to learn from the sacrificial gift of this godly woman.
3. A sacrificial gift means far more to God than gifts given out of surplus income, where the elements of sacrifice and faith are not required.

Paul shed light on the motive in giving which pleases God when he wrote this to the early believers in Corinth: "For if the willingness is there, the gift is acceptable according to what one has, not according to what he does not have." (2 Corinthians 8:12, NIV)

It is clear that either a very small or a very large gift can be totally pleasing to God. Our motivation for making the gift is what God looks at.

The following story is told about the wealthy industrialist and inventor, R. G. LeTourneau. When he was a boy, God led him to give a ten-dollar offering to missions. It so happened that ten dollars represented his total earnings, saved from doing various jobs. Years later when he told about this, a lady reportedly asked him this question: "Mr. LeTourneau, as a boy you trusted God enough to give

Him everything. Would you be willing to do that again today?" LeTourneau answered her, "Without a doubt!" His life was a living example of his answer. It was his practice to give ninety percent of his income to the cause of Christian growth and world evangelization.

Once a friend told me of his surprise when he saw LeTourneau's home in East Texas. At this time in LeTourneau's life, God had so blessed him financially that he could have afforded a palace, but he chose to live in a modest home similar to that of his neighbors. Both he and the widow in Jesus' day were motivated by the desire to put God first in their lives, and they expressed this desire through their maximum giving.

MAXIMUM GIVING

You may be asking, "What is maximum giving?" My reply is simple. The money we have is not from the government or our business, but from God. Therefore He alone can determine the maximum. "...for it is He who is giving you power to make wealth." (Deuteronomy 8:18) *God is our source.*

I vividly remember an incident that happened while we were enlarging our church building. This addition was supposed to cost $500,000, but before it was finished, it cost $600,000. To raise the additional money, thirty men sat together, among whom was a rather wealthy man. During the meeting he began to make excuses for the small pledge he originally had made. He also explained why he could not give more now. He basically said, "I have given all the money the Internal Revenue Service will *allow* me to give this year."

After the meeting, a good friend of his put his arm around the man's shoulders and whispered, "Tom, when are you going to stop giving the government's money away and start giving some of your own?" This man's understanding of maximum giving was not determined through prayer or by God's leading. His concept was based on the maximum tax-deductible benefit which the government would allow in a year's business.

Actually, more than half of the contributions this man generally gave would have otherwise been paid as taxes anyway, so the amount he was actually parting with was only a fraction of the dollars given.

It seems to me, after looking closely at the account of the poor widow's gift of two copper coins, that God is extremely pleased by the spirit of love that causes people to give *above* the government allowance for deductions on taxes. If we are looking to the government as our source, then we must never give above what the government allows us to give. But if we are looking to God as our source, we need to forget the maximum allowable for deduction and give as the Holy Spirit guides and prompts us. *God is our source!*

So far as I know, the United States is the only country in the world where gifts to the church are deductible from one's income tax. Would your giving pattern change if this law were changed? If so, why?

THE DISAPPOINTMENT OF RICHES

Scripture warns us in 1 Timothy 6:9 & 10 about the dangers of a desire to get rich:

"People who want to get rich fall into temptation and a trap and into many foolish and harmful desires that plunge men into ruin and destruction. For the love of money is a root of all kinds of evil. Some people, eager for money, have wandered from the faith and pierced themselves with many griefs." (NIV)

Yet despite these clear warnings, the heart of man naturally desires wealth, even though it harms his faith and hurts him physically and mentally. A most revealing message about this is tucked away in the book of Judges. This book is a record of failures, because during that period of time "every man did that which was right in his own eyes." (Judges 17:6, KJV) Many of God's people had fallen into paganism and idolatry and were no longer attempting to worship the true and living God.

In Judges 17:1-4, we read about a woman who had apparently been saving money to give to God. Then one day the money was missing. It had been stolen. Can you imagine how angry she became? The *idea* of anyone stealing God's money. She even pronounced a curse on that person. Later, the thief turned out to be her own son, so she tried to appease everyone involved by begging him to take all this money and build some idols for his shrine. The son refused and passed the money back to his mother, who then went to the silversmith and gave him two hundred pieces of silver to build the idols. But there were eleven hundred pieces of silver originally. She gave two hundred pieces away and kept nine hundred pieces for herself. This is typical of those who are not saved or who, like Lot, remain spiritually immature.

Most people grow up having a desire to become rich. They fail to realize what the Bible says about *the disappointment of riches.*

God sometimes opens up to us Scriptures that become turning points in our lives. These are times when a Biblical truth becomes practical and gives answers to real problems in our Christian experience. One passage that spoke to me in this way is the story of the rich young ruler (read Mark 10:17-27).

Jesus did not mean that a rich man who will sell all he has and give to the poor will consequently go to heaven. Salvation is never earned by divesting oneself of all one's possessions. However, this young man had a deep problem—*that of loving his money.* He was more devoted to his possessions than to God. Every man, rich or poor, must love God above possessions (or anything else in his life) if he desires to enter the kingdom of God.

But the "natural man" does *not* love God supremely. That is why Jesus gave an illustration of something that is impossible. He was saying that a man must be *perfect* to get to heaven, which is an impossibility, humanly speaking.

It is impossible to put a full-grown desert camel through the eye of a sewing needle. It is just as impossible for a rich man—a man in love with his money to the extent that he puts that money above all else, particularly Jesus Christ, to go to heaven. The man who trusts in riches in this instance is one who has an attitude which says, "This money is *mine*! I would rather have my money than Jesus Christ."

This type of man is actually demonstrating the sinfulness of his heart and proving that "all have sinned, and come short of the glory of God." (Romans 3:23, KJV) If this sin alone (loving money more than God) can keep an otherwise righteous man out of heaven, think of the spiritual damage it can cause in the life of a Christian who clings to his money.

Jesus did not say it is wrong to be wealthy. The problem is putting wealth *above* all else. Money is neither good nor bad; it is amoral. The sin consists in what the owner of the money allows it to do to his heart. Actual possession of wealth may have little to do with "loving money." A poor man can be just as guilty as a rich man when he loves his meager possessions more than God.

But God can change a man's heart. Jesus concluded this lesson on giving and salvation by saying that with men salvation is impossible, but not with God; for with God all things are possible. Despite man's sinful heart which keeps him out of heaven, God is able by His grace, through our faith in Jesus Christ, to provide the perfect righteousness His holiness demands.

Years ago one of the world's wealthiest men heard Billy Graham deliver a challenging message on the supremacy of Christ. Being deeply convicted by the Spirit of God, this man said to Dr. Graham, "I would give everything I own in exchange for the peace and assurance you possess."

Dr. Graham replied, "You can have salvation for nothing, but you cannot receive it in exchange for something. I know you would be willing to give any material possession to buy it, but that would be impossible. Only Christ could purchase salvation on our behalf, and this He did by giving His life on the cross."

When Jesus said, "For with God all things are possible," He was well aware that He was headed toward Calvary, where the impossible—righteous standing before God for unrighteous man—would be accomplished and made available to all who believe. One can almost feel the depth of His disappointment when the rich young ruler walked away.

In another situation Jesus told His audience, "Beware, and be on your guard against every form of greed; for not even when one has an abundance does his life consist of his possessions." (Luke 12:15)

This greed means a desire to have more and more, and it leads to taking advantage of or defrauding other people for gain.

Jesus continued to illustrate the futility of amassing and storing great wealth (read Luke 12:16-21).

The warnings are self-explanatory. You will note this time that we have a "certain rich man" who "began reasoning to himself." It is evident the man did not pray to God for direction about how to conserve his riches. His personal decision was to build bigger and bigger barns for himself. These decisions promoted his own selfish comfort, which is the exact opposite of a Christ-centered attitude.

I knew a man who spent his whole life building one fortune after another. He had little time to enjoy life, because he was always working on a new business opportunity to make more money. He literally built larger barns in which to store his goods. His giving to the Lord was limited, and his vision for winning souls for Christ was small. He never let himself think in that direction.

I tried many times to get him involved in Bible study and in going to meetings where the speakers would effectively expound the Word of God. His answer to me was always the same: "I am satisfied with what I am doing. Even if I knew more, I would not change now. Later, I plan to sell out my business and then go full-time for the Lord." This man died before he sold any of his properties.

Many new Christians begin their pilgrimage with the attitude that making and spending money is not a part of the Christian life. But when they received Christ as Savior, they actually gave Him a title deed to every hour of their day and every possession. This is what "lordship" means. When Christ died on the cross to purchase us and free us from the penalty of sin, He redeemed not only our spirits, but everything in our lives—including finances.

THREE GUIDELINES

For every disappointment which material possessions may bring, we find a positive solution pointed out in the Bible. When properly understood and properly managed, riches can provide much joy and be the means of accomplishing a great deal of essential ministry in the cause of Christ.

First, we must guard our hearts against "the love of riches." Solomon, an extremely wealthy man, once said, "Above all else, guard your heart, for it is the wellspring of life." (Proverbs 4:23, NIV)

Jesus spoke to this matter in Matthew 6:33: "Seek ye first the kingdom of God, and His righteousness; and all these things shall be added unto you." When our hearts are in love with the things that God is in love with, money will be no problem and riches will not become a disappointment in our lives.

On this matter of the heart's affection, Paul's word to the Christians of Colossae is most instructive: "If ye then be risen with Christ, seek those things which are above, where Christ sitteth on the right hand of God. Set your affection on things above, not on things on the earth." (Colossians 3:1-2, KJV) This kind of mindset will result in *sacrificial giving* rather than just big talk.

Second, we must be careful to do our giving for the right reason.

"Be careful not to do your 'acts of righteousness' before men, to be seen by them. If you do, you will have no reward from your Father in heaven. So when you give to the needy, do not announce it with trumpets, as the hypocrites do in the synagogues and on the streets, to be honored by men. I tell you the truth, they have received their reward in full. But when you give to the needy, do not let your left hand know what your right hand is doing, so that your giving may be in secret. Then your Father, who sees what is done in secret, will reward you." (Matthew 6:1-4, NIV)

Riches given for the wrong reason will bring great disappointment to the donor, because the act of giving will have no eternal consequences. The apostle John's comment summarizes why some people make a proud display of gifts: "They loved the praise of men more than the praise of God." (John 12:43, KJV)

Third, we must make giving our primary objective in obtaining wealth. The writer of Proverbs said, "Do not weary yourself to gain wealth, cease from your consideration of it. When you set your eyes upon it, it is gone. For wealth certainly makes itself wings, like an eagle that flies toward the heavens." (Proverbs 23:4 & 5)

Wealth is meant to be given away. When one attempts to possess it and cling to it, he finds, to his deep disappointment, that it flies away. A fire, a lawsuit, a depression, inflation, illness, divorce, wayward children, and a host of other familiar problems are the enemies of wealth. Giving is the friend of wealth, for with it comes joy and fulfillment rather than disappointment.

Both eventualities are pictured in Proverbs 11:28—"Whoever trusts in his riches will fall, but the righteous will thrive like a green leaf." (NIV)

Three simple guidelines, then, are: (1) Guard your hearts against the love of riches; (2) Be careful to give for the right reason; (3) Make giving a primary objective in obtaining wealth. These guidelines are enough to change a person's life.

PRACTICAL PRINCIPLES OF GIVING

Plan to Be Rich in Heaven. A major motivation behind giving on earth is to store up treasures in heaven. Again, recall that Jesus declared, "Do not store up for yourselves treasures on earth, where moth and rust destroy, and where thieves break in and steal. But store up for yourselves treasures in heaven...For where your treasure is, there your heart will be also." (Matthew 6:19-21, NIV)

If you really want to know where your heart is, look back over your cancelled checks for the last three years and see where your money has gone. This exercise may reveal more than you want to know! How much of your money is actually being stored up in heaven?

No matter what the affections of your heart may be, your checkbook will reveal them to you. Spending money unwisely may be foolish, but spending God's money without His consent is sin. Sooner or later, such a lifestyle will undermine our testimony for Christ and will adversely affect the quality of our lives.

Satan is eager to accommodate our fleshly desires and will provide moths, rust, and thieves in abundance to help dissipate and consume as much of God's money as possible. So resist Satan and invest your money in the safest place in the universe: heaven.

Give to Those Who Minister to You. We should support financially those who minister the Word of God to us, as Paul pointed out in 1 Corinthians 9:14 – "The Lord directed those who proclaim the gospel to get their living from the gospel" (see 1 Corinthians 9:7-14).

Plan for a Short Life. We are, in the language of a friend from Texas, "tenant farmers with a short-term lease." Job said, "My days are swifter than a weaver's shuttle." (Job 7:6) And the apostle James wrote, "You don't know what your life will be like tomorrow. You are just a vapor that appears for a little while and then vanishes away." (James 4:14) The brevity of life inspired Moses to write these words: "So teach us to number our days, that we may apply our hearts unto wisdom." (Psalm 90:12, KJV)

The person who plans to live each day to the fullest lives wisely. He will not leave things undone because of procrastination. He will seek to live one day at a time and get the most out of life.

"Redeeming the time" (Ephesians 5:16) is a practice the Lord commands because a spiritual battle is in progress, and every day we are moving closer to His appearing in glory. As evangelist Grady Wilson frequently said, "Whatever we are going to do for God, we had best do quickly."

Make Christ Lord of All. Jesus once taught a parable (Mark 4:1-20) which described four types of soil. One of the soil types contained thorns. After the seed of God's Word had been planted in this soil, those thorns continued to grow unhindered. Their devastating effect is described by Jesus in His explanation of the parable. He described those thorns as "the worries of the world, and the deceitfulness of riches, and the desires for other things." Their terrible result in our lives is that they "enter in and choke the Word, and it becomes unfruitful." (Mark 4:19)

A person can hear what God has to say about giving and start out with excellent intentions. But when he encounters worries, financial temptations, and the constant allurement of "other things," his first love for Christ may be choked out, and he becomes mediocre in his spiritual commitment.

Plan Ahead to Give. In 1 Corinthians 16:1 & 2, we learn that Christians should plan their giving ahead of time. "Now about the collection for God's people: do what I told the Galatian churches to do. On the first day of every week, each one of you should set aside a sum of money in keeping with his income, saving it up, so that when I come no collections will have to be made." (1 Corinthians 16:1 & 2, NIV)

These instructions are practical and easy to follow. Everyone was to participate and do his giving prior to Paul's arrival.

Give to Your Church. These particular gifts in 1 Corinthians 16 were for a mission project. Today, most of our gifts normally should go to a local church, provided that the church is preaching and applying the word of God in such a way that people are being saved, nourished, and instructed in the grace and knowledge of Christ.

Invest in People. People were Jesus' first concern. He gave Himself not for an institution, but for *people* of every kind and background. How can we follow His example in ministering through giving today? And how does this giving relate to storing up riches in heaven?

When we give to feed the poor, we are sharing a *testimony of the love of God* which can eventually open the door for us to share the gospel. Regardless of where God leads us to give, our objective should be not only to meet the immediate need but to save individual souls for eternity.

While it is a great privilege to be able to feed starving people physically, it is even better to teach them how to feed themselves spiritually. Having first demonstrated visibly the love of Christ, we can then share the gospel with them. The ultimate goal, of course, is to bring them to the saving knowledge of Christ our Savior. Jesus underscored the preeminence of the spiritual need of man in Matthew 4:4 when He quoted this Old Testament Scripture: "Man shall not live by bread alone, but by every word that proceedeth out of the mouth of God."

Let God Lead You. A consecrated believer, living under the control of the Spirit of God, will find direction from God regarding all of his giving—the amount of the gifts and who should receive them. The scriptural guidelines in this chapter are intended to be only an outline. The Holy Spirit will fill in the outline as He speaks to you personally. When you seriously want to know *who* to give to and *how much,* remember to start with *prayer.* Beginning each morning with prayer and Bible reading with a personal application will provide guidance not only in giving, but in other matters as well.

To carry out our good intentions, we should develop realistic questions to ask those who request our gifts of God's resources. Good stewardship demands that we understand where and how the Lord's money is being used.

Give Cheerfully. God's principle in giving to us or withholding from us is this: If we sow meagerly, we reap meagerly; if we sow generously, we reap generously. As Paul wrote in 2 Corinthians 9:6 & 7, "He who sows sparingly will also reap sparingly, and he who sows bountifully will also reap bountifully. So let each one give as he purposes in his heart, not grudgingly or of necessity; for God loves a cheerful giver." (NKJV)

God uses the farmer to teach us. If we give little—like the farmer who sows few seeds—we get little in return. If we give much—like the farmer who sows many seeds–we get much more in return.

We must make our own decision, under God's direction, about how much we are to give. We are not to be pushed or forced, but with a *willing heart* we should permit Him to set the amount. The Holy Spirit, whose job it is to instruct, train, and lead us in our decisions, will enlighten our minds. Then our gift will be eagerly given—so that we can hardly wait to sign the check.

Do you give with that kind of eagerness and joy? You should, for God loves a *cheerful* giver, one who purposes in his heart to give to Him, then does it gladly.

Give With Your Whole Heart. Armies have never won battles with halfhearted fighting men. The same is true in the spiritual realm. We give business, sports, travel, education, and sex our wholehearted attention, but many of us are satisfied with just "getting by" in our Christian lives. Yet God has given us this commandment: "Love the Lord your God with all your heart, and with all your soul, and with all your mind, and with all your strength." (Mark 12:30) Furthermore, God has promised: "You will seek me and find me when you seek me with all your heart." (Jeremiah 29:13, NIV) This is true in our giving as in all areas of our Christian life.

Give for God's Glory. Years ago I came to the conclusion that the word *glory* seemed to stand for an important doctrine in the Bible, though it was sometimes hard to understand.

The word has different meanings, but there is generally one idea which recurs whenever God's glory is discussed: Where God's glory is, *there is the presence of the Lord.* For example, Moses in Exodus 33 asked the Lord to show him His glory. In the same context God said, "My *presence* shall go with thee." (Exodus 33:14, KJV) Almost everywhere the term *glory* is used, the *presence* of the Lord is there too.

I am convinced that when we "glorify" God by giving, we are actually acknowledging His presence in the act itself. This is one reason why we should not give for the praise of men.

SUMMARY HIGHLIGHTS

The following principles summarize some of the main points we have examined in the Bible's teaching on giving:

• God owns everything. We do not have any absolute rights to ownership of anything, but we hold possessions "in trust" for God (Psalm 24:1).

• After giving God His rightful part—a tithe from our "first fruits"— we are to give in proportion to how God has blessed us, no matter what our income is. This refers to spiritual as well as material blessings.

• God's giving is tied to His *love.* God is love, and the greatest example of giving known to man is His giving His Son, Jesus Christ, to die on the cross for our sins. Because love gives, we as members of God's family must give. Because of the Holy Spirit within us, the love of God is active in our bodies; thus we are to give as God gave.

- Jesus said, "Give, and it shall be given unto you." (Luke 6:38, KJV) This is the principle on which God works, and this principle never varies. The opposite is true as well—withhold, and you will not receive.

- The basic principle of all giving is that GOD IS OUR SOURCE. He has in store for us all that we will ever need of anything. He has promised to "supply all of your need according to His riches in glory by Christ Jesus." (Philippians 4:19, KJV)

- We are instructed by Scripture to share our wealth with those who teach us God's Word (Galatians 6:6). This is the basic principle behind the practice of paying pastors and other full-time Christian workers.

- We must yield or present our bodies to Christ as a living sacrifice (Romans 12:1). This is total commitment on our part. We give everything back to God, who created us and gave us these gifts in the first place. This giving ourselves to God furnishes us with the power and desire to give His money for His work.

- We are to grow in grace continually—in everything. Our faith, witnessing, knowledge of God, love, and giving should grow stronger as we continually experience God's grace. The believer in Jesus Christ is never in a *status quo* situation. He is either advancing or sliding back.

- We give generously to those in need. This giving will be a testimony to others who will glorify God.

- From the early days in the Old Testament, God's people have come to worship bringing gifts. So giving is a form of worship. Do not come to church empty-handed, but bring your gifts to God.

CHAPTER 10

THANKSGIVING

Can a Christian thank God in all circumstances? Yes! Because "we know that all things work together for good to those who love God, to those who are called according to His purpose." (Romans 8:28, NKJV) We can thank Him for that truth, especially in our darkest and loneliest hours. He is not afraid of hard times and promised, "I will never leave you or forsake you." (Hebrews 13:5b, NKJV) One of the names used to describe our Lord is Immanuel. It means — God with us! And He always is.

You are never alone. In your highest moments of inspiration and the heaviest hours of your grief, He is with you. You are not a victim of your circumstances. The Lord said, "In this world you will have trouble. But take heart! I have overcome the world." (John 16:33b, NIV)

Thanksgiving is living in the very heart of *reality*. It is a *reality* that defies explanation outside our relationship with Christ. Those around you who do not know Christ are living outside of reality and are blind to the principles and resources the Lord made available to us when He overcame the world. This is why the Christian's optimism is often thought of as naive. It also explains why we often see society's values as selfish, cynical, and arbitrary.

Thanksgiving is based upon facts that cannot be changed and truth that brings light into darkness. The angel whose words we sing at Christmas said, "I bring you good news of a great joy...for today in the city of David there has been born for you a Savior." (Luke 2:10b & 11a) From that time until our time, the lives of those who have met the Savior have been seasoned with joy and thanksgiving.

JESUS' ATTITUDE TOWARD THANKFULNESS

From the beginning of Christ's earthly ministry, He looked for the attribute of thanksgiving in the lives of people. One day, as He was "on His way to Jerusalem, Jesus traveled along the border between Samaria and Galilee. As He was going into a village, ten men who had leprosy met Him. They stood at a distance and called out in a loud voice, 'Jesus, Master, have pity on us!' When He saw them He said, 'Go, show yourselves to the priests.' And as they went, they were cleansed. One of them, when He saw He was healed, came back, praising God in a loud voice. He threw Himself at Jesus' feet and thanked Him." (Luke 17:11-16a, NIV)

The high value the Lord attached to the words "thank you" is felt in His question to the Samaritan leper whom He had healed. "Were not all ten cleansed? Where are the other nine?" In life, you are either the one who gives thanks or one of the nine who do not. Either you appreciate His daily gifts, or you take them for granted. It is obvious from this passage that God both notices and is moved by our response.

The Lord Jesus was careful to give thanks and to set a proper example for us as God's children. When He fed the 4,000, He gave thanks (Matthew 15:36), and in private with the apostles at their parting meal (Matthew 26:27), He did the same. He lived with an attitude of thanksgiving and the awareness that every good and perfect gift comes from the Father (James 1:17).

Biblically, thanksgiving means expressing gratitude to God, not for who He is, but for what He has done. Part of man's sin problem can be clearly seen in his thankless attitude. Paul describes this problem: "For since the creation of the world God's invisible qualities – His eternal power and divine nature – have been clearly seen, being understood from what has been made, so that men are without excuse. For although they knew God, they neither glorified Him as God nor gave thanks to Him, but their thinking became futile and their foolish hearts were darkened." (Romans 1:20 & 21, NIV)

BARRIERS TO GRATITUDE

Large blocks of the world's population developed false religions and philosophies which destroyed the very basis for offering sincere thanks to God in prayer. One segment built its religious philosophy around what they call "karma," which simply means "works." Because they believe that their good works produce their blessings, logically they can thank themselves rather than God for all that He gives them. Those religions which believe in fate or chance are equally thankless because there is no one to thank. Who has ever seen or talked with "fate"?

Those who embrace agnosticism or atheism cannot express thanks to anything but nature and impersonal forces which they do not fully understand. Expressing gratitude with that unrealistic mindset is not only unlikely, but illogical.

Lastly, there are those who relentlessly express a form of religious gratitude, but to a god of their own design. Their rigid formalism is expressed with legalistic punctuality. Tragically, such thanksgiving is more like a cuckoo clock, mechanically making the right sounds at the right times. Because the Holy Spirit is not there, the reality of love and a personal relationship with God (which He, too, desires) are absent. As the Apostle Paul taught, lack of thanksgiving is an evidence that true worship is missing.

Beyond man-made religions and philosophies, another barrier to our saying "thank you" seems to be innate in our human nature. It is the fear of admitting our own inadequacy. Our unspoken understanding goes like this: "If I have to thank God for something, it means that I cannot do it for myself. Therefore, I must be inadequate." This is true, though our pride makes it extremely hard to accept. We are both physically and spiritually inadequate from the very first days of our lives. Physically, we are born depending upon others and we die depending on others. To deepen your understanding of this reality, simply visit a hospital nursery and a convalescent home on the same day.

If we who are created in God's image feel the need to hear the words, "thank you," why does it surprise us that He wants to hear those words as well? If for no other reason, He desires to hear them for our sake, because expressions of appreciation are signs of increasing maturity. When you were a child, at first your parents taught you to say "thank you" whether you felt like it or not. It was only as you matured that the expenditure of other people's effort, time, and material goods became truly significant. A sincere "thank you" is an evidence of growing understanding.

RESULTS OF INGRATITUDE

Ingratitude, on any level, strains a relationship. I personally experienced the sting of ingratitude during my junior year in high school. A houseguest from another country, who had been a casual family acquaintance, wrote asking if he could visit us on his upcoming trip to Texas. He received an enthusiastic "yes" from all of us. To insure his happiness while in San Angelo, it was decided that I would sleep on the couch so he could use my bedroom. In addition, he was to drive my car. Learning of his interest in horses, we arranged for him to ride a good quarterhorse belonging to a neighboring rancher. Other courtesies were planned, including a party honoring him and a trip to Austin to meet the Governor.

His one week stay stretched into two, then three, and finally six! During all this time, our bird-watching, military judo instructor, atheist guest never offered to buy anyone so much as a cup of coffee. However, he did manage to throw me across the living room, wreck the car, and totally lather our friend's horse. More importantly, two words were missing from his otherwise extensive English vocabulary: "Thank you!"

Psalm 24:1 says, "The earth is the Lord's, and all it contains, the world, and those who dwell in it." How embarrassing it would be for otherwise polite people to see themselves as God sees them. They drink His water, eat His food, and enjoy His hospitality to the fullest extent, never realizing that the sky above their heads is His and the grass beneath their feet is the carpet of a beautiful house which belongs to Him. Ironically, He hears His name profaned millions of times every hour, but He seldom hears the words, "Thank you." Even when people are happy or surprised, His name is used as an oath. No human host alive would tolerate such abusive treatment in his own living room.

The opposite of thanksgiving is ingratitude. Ingratitude, carried to its ultimate conclusion, is not only to be unthankful but to rudely ignore the host himself. The beginning of Christian growth is to inwardly feel and express appreciation to your heavenly Host.

WHEN TO SAY "THANK YOU"

"In everything give thanks, for this is God's will for you in Christ Jesus." (1 Thessalonians 5:18) Based upon Paul's words to the early Christians, it is probably more appropriate to ask, "When shouldn't I give thanks?" It is clear that the very attitude of our lives should be one of consistent joy and thanksgiving, regardless of our outward circumstances.

Since Paul was led to pen these words, it is important to know that his walk was consistent with his talk. When he and Silas were imprisoned in Philippi, the Scripture says, "They were praying and singing hymns of praise to God" (Acts 16:25) as their fellow prisoners listened. The fact that their feet were in stocks and that they had been beaten with rods earlier in the afternoon did not alter their commitment to giving thanks. Less mature people under similar circumstances would probably have asked, "God, is this how You treat Your best servants?" Instead, Paul and Silas sang and prayed in faith, keeping their focus upon His adequacy in every human situation. When the earthquake came that night and the prison doors swung open, the greater miracle had already occurred within them. They had overcome that tendency of human nature and given praise by faith.

The proper time for an attitude of thanks is—always! But expressing our feelings of gratitude often comes as a result of receiving a new insight. When Nebuchadnezzar, the most powerful man in the world, saw God's miraculous delivery of Shadrach,

Meshach and Abednego, whom Nebuchadnezzar had thrown into a fiery furnace, the king was in awe. He prayed, "Blessed be the God of Shadrach, Meshach, and Abednego, who has sent His angel and delivered His servants who put their trust in Him." (Daniel 3:28) This was an instance where thanksgiving and adoration naturally blended together.

As you pray, this will often occur together in your life as well. In one moment you will be praising God for who He is, and in the next you will be thanking Him for the wonderful things He has done.

WHAT TO BE THANKFUL FOR

For many years I made the spiritual mistake of taking normal things for granted. But a close friend told me of his experience with the late E. Stanley Jones, one of the best-known missionaries of our century. This godly man shared Christ with great power and clarity throughout much of India.

One day as my friend, Dr. A. B. Masilamani, and Dr. Jones were traveling together, Masi was surprised to see tears in his eyes and asked, "Why are you crying?" "Thanksgiving," said Dr. Jones. "You see, Masi, these legs have carried me up and down the mountains of India for many years, and these hands have been more than faithful in accomplishing what I wanted them to."

Then he thoughtfully patted his knee and complimented it for having worked so well. Thoughtfully, he said, "Before long I will be receiving a new body and leaving this old friend behind." Little by little, Dr. Jones thanked God for his entire body, one limb at a time.

Most of us never thank God for our eyes, limbs, and ability to function until we have undergone a tragic loss which causes us to appreciate what we had before. May we have the wisdom of this aged saint who, "always giving thanks for all things," (Ephesians 5:20) thanked God for his body while he still had it. When you start thanking God for normal things, gratitude becomes a way of life. Soon you will become aware of things you have never appreciated before.

Learning what to thank God for isn't really difficult. The key is

in understanding that everything you have is provided as a stewardship from Him. This simply means that everything you possess is
on loan from God.

THANKING GOD FOR PROVISION

God is watching with great interest to see how you will respond
to the privilege of life. The Scripture says if you are faithful in a few
things, He will make you ruler over many (Matthew 25:21). Since
He is the source of our provision, when He finds our response to be
in accordance with His teachings, He can trust us with increased
responsibilities and opportunities.

As this relates to material provision, the Lord said, "Seek first
the kingdom of God and His righteousness, and all these things shall
be added unto you." (Matthew 6:33, NKJV) This promise of provision is accompanied by the balance of divine wisdom which is
explained in many parts of the Scriptures. When a parent spoils a
child or denies him the privilege of learning the value of honest
labor, the parent's provision is no longer a blessing but a curse.
God's desire is to make us spiritually strong, healthy, and enthusiastic about life. Like any good parent, He must carefully evaluate
how many material blessings we need.

You are God's child, and He wants to bless you just as much as
you will let Him! He doesn't want to hurt you—He wants to help,
and He knows what you need, not what you think you need, even
before you ask. Did Jesus not say, "…your Father knows what you
need, before you ask Him?" (Matthew 6:8b) The testimony of the
psalmist remains ever true, "I have been young, and now I am old;
yet I have not seen the righteous forsaken, or his descendants
begging bread." (Psalm 37:25)

As a seminary student, I learned this important lesson one
unforgettable morning in Taiwan. I had been traveling for two
months with a team of eight other students, preaching evangelistic
crusades around the world. Weeks before, when I left, we were still
$2,500 short for the overseas ministry, but there was no doubt that
the team was supposed to go. In Taiwan, it was quite a shock to
discover that each of us thought the others still had some money. It

was awkward to share with our missionary host that all we had left was our plane tickets home. At least they would provide meals on the plane!

That morning we prayed that God would give us a definite answer as to whether we should leave immediately or continue with the two exciting weeks of ministry which had been planned. At noon, a cable arrived with the following message: "LETTER TO MAXI JARMAN LOST BY SECRETARY STOP JUST REFOUND STOP SENT $2,500 STOP HE SAID I HOPE IT WILL NOT BE TOO LATE TO BE OF SOME ASSISTANCE STOP."

To say we were thankful would be an understatement. The arrival of the money was not only perfectly timed but his check was for the *exact* remaining need! Our letter to Mr. Jarman had only mentioned the larger amount required for the entire budget. "Faithful is He who calls you, and He also will bring it to pass." (1 Thessalonians 5:24) God will never call you to carry out a project which He will not staff, empower, and fund!

THANKING GOD IN TIMES OF STRESS

Finances are one of God's major ways of dealing with us in spiritual growth, because so much of man's time is devoted to making and spending money. For this reason, some of your greatest tests and most thrilling moments of joy will be related to the possessions which money affords.

A businessman who is a close friend told me how he learned to give thanks in the school of patience. He owned valuable property in a strategic location. Because of his convictions concerning alcoholism, he turned down a substantial offer to build and lease a restaurant which would serve liquor. Then he refused to sell the land for a large eight screen theater which, among other things, would show R-rated films. Like everyone else, he could have used the money, but not at the cost of contributing toward alcoholism or moral decay.

I was not surprised to learn that he was in the midst of negotiating a much better contract using the land for a beneficial purpose. His thanksgiving was accompanied by the peace of mind that comes from letting "patience have its perfect work, that you may be perfect and complete, lacking nothing." (James 1:4, NKJV)

Health either has been or will be an important area for thanksgiving in your life. Sometimes the occasion for joy is for yourself, and sometimes on behalf of others. In either case, as the Scripture says, "It is good to give thanks to the Lord." (Psalm 92:1)

It is hard to imagine giving thanks for mononucleosis, but I have learned that there are times when you can almost shout for joy over such a diagnosis. Our oldest daughter, Heidi, had not been well for over six months. She had been to several doctors and had had a bone scan, a brain scan, and an encephalogram. The doctors had prepared us for the worst, because they feared the diagnosis would be epilepsy, a brain tumor, or multiple sclerosis. Heidi had subconsciously committed herself to get ready to "leave for heaven." The final straw (and answer too!) was an alarming swelling on both sides of her neck. That was the clue the doctors needed to order a simple blood test which confirmed an unusual and long-lasting form of mononucleosis.

Though she had to miss an overseas trip on which she had been invited to play the harp with the Youth Orchestra, she fully shared our joy and thanked God for these circumstances. For her, giving thanks was an evidence of growing maturity in her faith. For us, it was sheer appreciation for His guidance which we had earnestly sought as parents.

TAKE TIME TO LISTEN

Some years ago, I felt there was a need for a certain kind of Christian music. With little or no specific prayer, I dove into the project. After six months of diligent effort, the manuscript was ready to mail to a potential publisher.

In anticipation of calling a music publisher in Chicago, I went to my bedroom for a time of private prayer. In retrospect, it is clear that my attitude could not have pleased God, because there was no real adoration for Him in my heart—only adoration for the music. My words sounded pious as I reminded Him that His name was mentioned throughout the music and that the songs were dedicated in His honor.

Prayer is a spiritual dialogue, and in our minds God is faithful to carry out His part of the conversation. The key is stopping to listen. On this occasion, the communication was unmistakably clear: "Billie, you say the music belongs to Me. If it does, you won't care what I choose to do with it, will you?"

My immediate reaction was one of puzzlement. I began to gently argue my position: "Lord, wouldn't You like to bless the music for Your glory and make it sell thousands of copies?" This was the beginning of a painful six-week struggle, during which I was aware that I could not call Chicago and be in God's will until I was fully prepared to thank Him equally for a "yes" or "no" answer from the publisher.

Only when my focus turned away from the music, and only when His will became more important to me than my aspirations, did the victory come. The music was never published.

Years later, I found the manuscript in a drawer. Curiously, I re-read the words of each song, and thanked God again—this time for a different reason. The music was so shallow and faddish that it was totally unworthy of bearing His name!

The deeper lesson that came from this experience has been of genuine benefit ever since. The objective of the Christian life is living in the kind of obedience that demonstrates our love. We are not to set out on projects of our own and then ask God to bless them. He will never rubber stamp our will. However, when music or anything else is born in heaven and He commissions us to move in a certain direction, the simplest obedience will be accompanied by amazing results.

This reminds me of an incident that occurred while I was serving as a youth evangelist. We had been praying that God would enable us to increase our giving for His work. Our five dollars a week seemed such a small tithe in view of the tremendous needs throughout the world. The Lord's response to that prayer was to ask me to give Him something with the stipulation that I would never personally use any of the income which might be derived from that gift. What He wanted, and what I gave Him that day, was a song which had been written out of a haunting concern for the loneliness of lost people in huge urban areas like New York, London, and Tokyo. Though my salary remained the same, miraculously, "Lonely Voices" enabled us to increase our giving that year from $5 to $55 per week!

In one instance through music, He taught us to thank Him for a "no." In the other we have been privileged to thank Him for almost twenty years for a "yes."

> The adventure of living by faith is the gateway to a life of thanksgiving. Faith doesn't beg or plead; it patiently listens and then obediently responds to the inner prompting of the Holy Spirit's leadership. As Christians have always emphasized, faith says, "Thank you." When God makes a promise, faith believes it, accepts it, and moves ahead in gratitude. We are to "Enter His gates with thanksgiving." (Psalm 100:4)

LESSONS
IN
CHRISTIAN
DISCIPLESHIP

1 – 9

ROOTED AND BUILT UP IN HIM

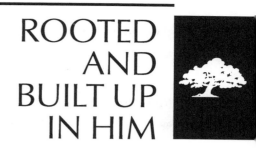

"As you therefore have received Christ Jesus the Lord, so walk in Him, having been firmly rooted and now being built up in Him and established in your faith, just as you were instructed, and overflowing with gratitude." (Colossians 2:6 & 7)

Lessons In Christian Discipleship is designed to communicate God's Word practically and systematically. The goal of these lessons is to assist you in your desire to:

> *Know* God better
> *Understand* the Bible
> *Apply* God's Word in your daily life

PREPARATION FOR THIS STUDY

1. Use an up to date translation of the Bible.
2. Set aside a definite time and place to study.
3. Begin your study with prayer, asking God to be your teacher.
4. After reading the question and the corresponding Bible passage, answer the question in you own words.
   Each Bible passage will give the book, chapter, and verse. For example, John 3:16 refers to the book of John, Chapter 3, verse 16.
5. The goal of your study will be a *changed life!* Think about each subject you study and seek to make personal.
6. Share what you learn with others.

Throughout your study you will see this symbol:

This section is to designed to stimulate your thinking about a Scriptural passage or principle. Prayerfully meditate on these questions. Remember, the purpose of Bible study is to become more like Jesus, so focus on your personal actions, attitudes, and thought life.

Ask the Lord to help you truly know Him as a result of these studies...

1. **The New Relationship**
2. **Putting Christ First**
3. **The Devotional Life**
4. **Prayer—Evidence of Dependency**
5. **Sharing Christ With Others**
6. **God Our Father**
7. **The Ministry of the Holy Spirit**
8. **The Importance of God's Word**
9. **The Church—A Supportive Fellowship**

"So let us know,
let us press on to know the Lord...."
(Hosea 6:3)

LESSON ONE
THE NEW RELATIONSHIP

1

"You are all sons of God through faith in Christ Jesus."
(Galatians 3:26, NIV)

HIS CHILD FOREVER

When you asked Jesus Christ to be your Lord and Savior, you established a new relation with God and became His child. Because of that new relationship, you can enjoy certain wonderful promises! One benefit of being His child is the security of knowing you will never lose that relationship.

1. What promises does Jesus make to every child of God?
   John 10:27-29 _____

   _____

   _____

   1 John 2:25 _____

   _____

2. Describe your inheritance as a Christian. *1 Peter 1:3&4* _____

   _____

   _____

3. Why can you be secure in your relationship with God?
   1 Peter 1:5 _____

   _____

Jude 24 & 25 _____

_____

_____

4. What truths regarding eternal life do you see in 1 John 5:11-13?

_____

_____

_____

_____

_____

PEACE WITH GOD

"Therefore having been justified by faith, we have peace with God through our Lord Jesus Christ." (Romans 5:1)

Jesus' sacrificial death on the cross for your sins was complete in every sense. Nothing else is needed or can be added. His sacrifice fully paid for all your sins — past, present, and future!

5. Read Colossians 2:13 & 14.

    How does verse 13 describe your life before becoming a Christian? _____

    What did Lord do with your sins? *Verses 13 & 14* _____

    _____

    _____

    _____

6. Ephesians 1:7 is a summary of God's redemptive plan.

    Write this verse in your own words: _____

    _____

    _____

    _____

7. How is your relationship with God described in Romans 8:1?

    _____

    _____

    _____

8. What attitudes can now characterize your relationship with
    God? *Hebrews 10:19-22* _____

    _____

    The Biblical picture of your relationship with God is walking
    together. *"As you therefore have received Christ Jesus the Lord,
    so walk in Him."* (Colossians 2:6)

9. Read 1 John 1:5-10 and answer the following questions:
    What is "walking in the light"? *Verses 5 & 6* _____

    _____

    _____

    What are the results of "walking in the light"? *Verse 7* _____

    _____

    _____

    Do Christians consistently "walk in the light"? *Verses 8-10*

    _____

    When a Christian sins—walks in darkness—what should he do?
    Verse 9 _____

    _____

    Confession literally means *to say the same thing
    about something.* When a person confesses his sin,
    he should have the same attitude toward that sin that
    God has toward it.

10. What was David's response to sin in his own life? *Psalm 32:5*

    What was God's response to David's confession? _____

✝   *What is the relationship between Christ's death on the cross and our experience of peace with God?* _____

THE HOLY SPIRIT

The Holy Spirit is God Himself. He has been active on earth since creation. Before the Lord Jesus ever came, The Holy Spirit was already active in people's lives. During the earthly ministry of Jesus, He worked uniquely through the person of Christ. Since Jesus' return to the Father, every Christian has enjoyed a very special relationship with God the Holy Spirit.

11. When you became a Christian, what did the Holy Spirit do?
    1 Corinthians 3:16 _____
    1 Corinthians 6:19 & 20 _____

12. How long does the Holy Spirit remain in believers?
    John 14:16 & 17 _____

13. What does the Holy Spirit do after He comes to live within you?
    John 14:25 & 26 _____

    John 16:13 & 14 _____

14. What is available to every Christian through the Holy Spirit?
    Acts 1:8 _____

    _____

    Galatians 5: 22 & 23 _____

    _____

✝ *Who is the Holy Spirit to you personally?* _____

    _____

    _____

    _____

    _____

EVIDENCE OF YOUR NEW RELATIONSHIP

"Therefore, if anyone is in Christ, he is a new creation; the old has gone, the new has come." (2 Corinthians 5:17, NIV)

15. What evidence demonstrates your new relationship with God?
    Acts 4:20 _____

    _____

    1 Peter 2:2 _____

    _____

    1 Peter 4:3 & 4 _____

    _____

    1 John 2:3 _____
    1 John 3:14 _____

16. What was the evidence of conversion in these men:
    Man from Decapolis? *Mark 5:18-20* _____

    _____

    _____

Zaccheus? *Luke 19:8 & 9* _____

_____

_____

Saul? *Acts 9:20-22* _____

_____

_____

Philippian jailer? *Acts 16:30-34* _____

_____

_____

What evidence of conversion can you thank God for in your own experience? Briefly describe: _____

_____

_____

_____

_____

_____

EMPHASIS: You can know for certain that you belong to the family of God. Discuss the following topics from this study:

1. *His Child Forever*—Why is it important for you to have the security that you will actually belong to God forever?

2. *The Holy Spirit*—How does the work of the Holy Spirit positively affect your daily life?

SUMMARY

If you have believed in the Lord Jesus Christ, and have received Him by faith, then you have entered into a new relationship with God. You are His child forever. Nothing you do will ever change that eternal relationship. You can enjoy peace with God through the blood of Jesus Christ, and can walk in the light. The Holy Spirit lives in you and will work in you forever. The evidence of the new relationship in your life will help you gain assurance that you belong to God.

LESSON TWO PUTTING CHRIST FIRST 2

". . . If anyone would come after Me, he must deny himself, and take up his cross daily and follow Me. For whoever wants to save his life will lose it, but whoever loses his life for Me will save it."
(Luke 9:23 & 24, NIV)

LORD OF ALL

Jesus Christ is Lord universally. Regardless of how people respond to Him, eternity will reveal that He holds all authority.

1. What position has God given Jesus? *Acts 2:36* _____

_____

2. Read Colossians 1:15-18. How is Jesus Christ described?
*Verse 15*_____

In the following verses how is Christ's Lordship manifested?
Verse 16 _____
Verse 17 _____

_____

_____

Verse 18 _____

_____

_____

_____

3. What is Christ's position? *Ephesians 1:20-23*

Verse 20 _____

_____

Verse 21 _____

_____

Verse 22 _____

_____

4. What should every person acknowledge about Jesus Christ?

Philippians 2:9-11 _____

_____

Why? *Verse 11* _____

_____

> In *all* Christians, Christ is *present.*
> In *some* Christians, Christ is *prominent.*
> In a *few* Christians, Christ is *preeminent.*

LORD BY PURCHASE

Jesus Christ is Lord, not only because of who He is , but also because of what He did.

5. Using a dictionary, write the meaning of the word "redeem."

   _____

   _____

   _____

   _____

6. To what were you enslaved before you received Christ?
   Romans 6:6, 17 & 18 _____

   _____

   _____

How did being a slave of sin affect you personally?

   _____

   _____

   _____

   _____

   _____

7. What happened that released you from slavery?
   1 Corinthians 6:19 & 20 _____

   _____

8. What was the price paid for you? *1 Peter 1:18 & 19* _____

   _____

   _____

In the Bible, every man without Christ is pictured as a slave —
being owned by someone else. Jesus Christ *redeemed* us. He
purchased us out of the slave market of sin.

9. What is God's purpose in redeeming you?
    2 Corinthians 5:15 _____

    _____

    Galatians 4:3-5 _____

    _____

    Titus 2:14 _____

    _____

*Why do you think so many people never allow Jesus
Christ to be in first place of their daily lives?* _____

_____

_____

_____

_____

_____

Do you think any of these reasons are valid? Explain:

_____

_____

_____

*Why should you give Jesus Christ first place in your daily life?*_____

_____

_____

_____

THE TOUCH OF THE MASTER'S HAND

'Twas battered and scarred, and the auctioneer
    Thought it scarcely worth his while
To waste much time on the old violin,
    But he held it up with a smile.
"What am I bidden, good folk?" he cried,
    "Who'll start the bidding for me?
"A dollar—a dollar—then two, only two—
    "Two dollars, and who'll make it three?
"Going for three..." But no—
    From the room far back, a gray-haired man
Came forward and picked up the bow,
    Then, wiping the dust from the old violin.
And tightening the loosened strings,
    He played a melody pure and sweet
    As a caroling angel sings.

The music ceased, and the auctioneer,
    With a voice that was quiet and low,
Said, "NOW what am I bid for the old violin?"
    And he held it up with the bow.
"A thousand dollars—and who'll make it two?
    "Two thousand—and who'll make it three?
"Three thousand once— three thousand twice—
    "And going—and gone," cried he..
The people cheered, but some of them cried,
    "We do not understand.

"What changed its worth?" Quick came the reply,
"The touch of the Master's hand."

And many a man with life out of tune,
    And battered and scarred with sin,
Is auctioned cheap to a thoughtless crowd,
    Much like the old violin.
A "mess of pottage"—a glass of wine,
    A game—and he travels on:
He is going once—and going twice—
    He's going—and almost gone!
But the Master comes, and the foolish crowd
    Never can quite understand
The worth of a soul and the change that's wrought
    BY THE TOUCH OF THE MASTER'S HAND

—Myra Brooks

ALTERNATIVES TO PUTTING CHRIST FIRST

Many will admit that Jesus Christ deserves to be preeminent in their thoughts and plans, but in reality they do not submit to Him. Without submission to Christ, the quality of their daily experience will resemble that of a non-Christian.

10. The following chart aligns three types of men with their corresponding lifestyles. Look up the verses and list the types of men and a brief description of the way they live:

Types Of Men	Lifestyles Described
1 Corinthians 2:14 Type: _____	1 Corinthians 6:9-11
1 Corinthians 3:1 Type: _____	Hebrews 5:11-13
1 Corinthians 2:15 Type: _____	Galatians 5:22 & 23

11. How often should we make the decision to do the Lord's will?
    Luke 9:23 _____

12. What commitment is each Christian urged to make?
    Romans 12:1 & 2 _____
    _____

What does this verse mean to you personally? _____

_____

_____

_____

_____

KEEPING CHRIST FIRST

Believers experience daily temptation. Each of us has the ability to do both good and evil. We have two natures—the old sinful nature and the new nature of Christ. These two natures each strive for control of your decisions and actions. Putting Christ first means choosing to be governed by Him daily.

13. What are the results of living in the flesh (sinful nature)?
    1 Corinthians 3:1-3 _____

    _____

    _____

14. Describe the conflict that occurs in each Christian:
    Galatians 5:16-18 _____

    _____

15. How can this conflict be resolved? *Romans 13:14* _____

    _____

    _____

    _____

    How can you do this? _____

    _____

    _____

    _____

Meditate on Mark 8:34-38 and list the insight you see concerning the priority of Christ in your own life:

_____

_____

_____

_____

_____

PUTTING CHRIST FIRST

Putting Christ first does not necessarily mean entering vocational Christian service, but it does mean yielding to His will in every area of life. The real issue is learning to trust and desire His will instead of your own.

16. Read the passages of scripture on the following page, and name each area of priority using the topics below. Put a check mark beside each issue in which you are currently seeking to do God's will instead of your own:

career	family	friends
future	health	money
possessions	self	time
dating/marriage		

Passage	Priority Area	Personal Examination
1 Kings 11:1-4		
Matthew 4:18-22		
Matthew 10:37		
Luke 9:23		
Luke 12:15-21		
Luke 18:18-23		
2 Corinthians 6:14 & 15		
2 Corinthians 12:7-10		
Ephesians 5:15-17		
James 4:13-15		

In what areas do you have the greatest struggle in putting Christ first? _____

_____

_____

_____

_____

How does this struggle manifest itself? _____

_____

_____

_____

What will you need to do in order to give Christ first place in this area? _____

_____

_____

_____

17. Romans 12:1 & 2 describes the commitment God is calling us to make. How is a life described when it is truly submitted to Christ? *Verse 2* _____

_____

In your own words, describe the primary changes that will begin to take place in your life as you become "good and acceptable and perfect." _____

_____

_____

_____

_____

_____

EMPHASIS: The issue of putting Christ first centers on doing His will instead of your own. Discuss these questions together:

1. What does it personally mean to you for Jesus Christ to be of first priority in your daily life?

2. Why do we continue to struggle with the priority issue, even after we have submitted to Jesus as Lord initially?

SUMMARY

God has made Jesus Lord. He is Lord by creation and because He has redeemed you from the slave market of sin. The alternatives to putting Christ first are to live a worldly life or be a carnal Christian defeated by sin. As you submit once and for all to Christ and place every area of your life under His control, you will experience God's best for your life. Will you pray to God right now and yield your entire life to His total control? Will you pray, "God, use me anyway, anytime, anywhere?"

LESSON THREE THE DEVOTIONAL LIFE **3**

Few Christians plan to mature beyond a casual relationship with God. For many, that relationship could simply be characterized as going to church on Sunday, praying when a problem arises and occasionally reading a few verses of Scripture. A vital day-by-day relationship with God will never develop on that basis. The Bible says, "*. . . draw near to God and He will draw near to you.*" (James 4:8)

To know God better, you must plan to spend time enjoying the privilege of His fellowship!

THE PURPOSE OF THE DEVOTIONAL LIFE

1. What are some attitudes you see in the Psalmist's relationship with God?

    Psalm 42:1 & 2 _____

    _____

    _____

    Psalm 62:5 _____

    _____

    _____

    _____

Psalm 63:1 _____

_____

2. Read the verses below and match each one with the appropriate word. Example: Psalm 105:4 matches "seeking" God.

| Psalm 95:6 | 1 John 1:9 | Psalm 113:1 |
| Psalm 27:14 | Matthew 7:7 & 8 | Psalm 75:1 |

Psalm 105:4	Seeking	G
	Waiting on	
	Praising	O
	Worshipping	
	Thanking	
	Confessing	D
	Asking	

3. What should lead you to worship Him? *Revelation 4:11*

_____

4. How do you worship Him? *John 4:23 & 24* _____

_____

In your opinion, what does it mean to "worship God in spirit and in truth"? _____

_____

_____

_____

5. What is every Christian's calling? *1 Corinthians 1:9* _____

_____

> "One of the most amazing truths of Scripture is that the almighty sovereign God longs to have intimate, personal fellowship with every child of His. An equally amazing truth is that throughout history so few of His followers ever avail themselves of this glorious soul-filling experience."

EXAMPLES IN SCRIPTURE

One of the notable characteristics of men and women of God throughout history has been their commitment to know Him. Many of them rose early in the morning to seek Him. They lived in many different places at different times, but they all had one thing in common—their hunger for God.

6. Complete the chart below:

Passage	Person	Time of Day	Place	Activity
Genesis 19:27				
Exodus 34:2				
Psalm 5:3				
Daniel 6:10				
Mark 1:35				

What personal application can you make from these examples? _____

_____

_____

_____

THROUGH HIS WORD

" '...Take to your heart all the words with which I am warning you today, which you shall command your sons to observe carefully, even all the words if this law. For it is not an idle word for you; indeed it is your life...' " (Deuteronomy 32:46 & 47)

7. According to each of the following verses, what is the purpose of God's Word?

    John 5:39 _____

    John 20:31 _____

    _____

8. Read 2 Timothy 3:16 & 17. How does the Word of God help you learn to walk with God? _____

    _____

    _____

9. Read 2 Peter 1:3 & 4

    What has God has already given you? *Verse 3* _____

    _____

    How do you obtain what He has given you? *Verse 3* _____

    _____

    What is the purpose of God's promises? *Verse 4* _____

    _____

10. How does God's Word become a vital part of your life?

     Joshua 1:8 _____

     _____

     _____

     Psalm 119:9-11 _____

     _____

     _____

11. The Word of God is sometimes compared to everyday items which help us understand its purpose. Look up the verses and complete the chart below:

Verse	Comparison	Purpose
Psalm 119:105	light, lamp	to guide us
Psalm 19:10, 11		
Jeremiah 23:28, 29		
John 15:3 and Ephesians 5:26		
Ephesians 6:17 and Hebrews 4:12		
1 Peter 2:2		

Why is God's Word important to you? _____

_____

_____

_____

THROUGH PRAYER

"But He Himself would often slip away to the wilderness and pray." (Luke 5:16)

12. Why should you pray?
    1 Samuel 12:23 _____

    _____

    Matthew 26:41 _____

    _____

    Hebrews 4:16 _____

    _____

13. What does God promise when you pray?
    Jeremiah 33:3 _____

    _____

    John 14:13 & 14 _____

    _____

14. After reading each verse, select the correct answer from the list below and write it out beside the verse:

    Verse

    Psalm 66:18 _____
    Matthew 21:22 _____
    John 15:7 _____
    James 4:2 _____
    James 4:3 _____
    1 John 3:22 _____

    Answer

ask	ask believing
obey and please Him	no unconfessed sin
ask with right motives	abiding in Christ

15. Based upon Philippians 4:6 & 7, what should you pray about?

_____

_____

16. Listed below are five aspects of prayer. Draw a line from each
    aspect to the matching verse:

Aspects	**Verses**
A doration Praising God for who He is	1 Thessalonians 5:18
C onfession Agreeing with God about Your Sin	John 16:24
T hanksgiving Expressing Gratitude to God for What He has Done	1 Samuel 12:23
I ntercession Praying for the Needs of Others	1 John 1:9
P etition Praying for Your Personal Needs	Psalm 34:1

✝ *Having considered these verses, what changes do you
plan to make in your personal prayer life?* _____

_____

_____

_____

_____

_____

_____

How do you plan to start? _____

_____

_____

_____

CONTENT OF THE DEVOTIONAL LIFE

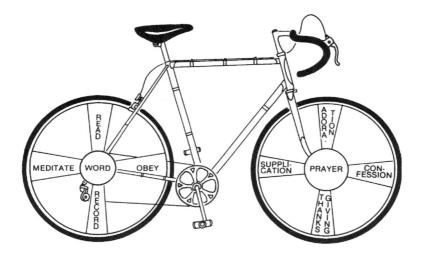

17. The devotional life can be graphically portrayed by the bicycle illustration above. The wheels represent the word and prayer. What observations about the devotional life can you make from this illustration?

_____

_____

_____

_____

_____

_____

_____

_____

MAINTAINING A VITAL DEVOTIONAL LIFE

Consistency is the primary problem faced by those seeking God. It is possible to be consistent and to make the devotional life a part of your lifestyle.

1. **A Basic Decision** – Your desire to meet with God will sometimes fluctuate with your feelings. The decision to meet with Him regardless of how you feel will help you become dependable and successful.

2. **Right Priority** – Jesus said, *"Seek first the kingdom of God and His righteousness...."* (Matthew 6:33) Nothing else should be more important in your daily schedule than your time with the Lord.

3. **Biblical Goal** – God has called you to fellowship with Christ and wants you to know Him. Your personal goal can now be to worship and enjoy Him. Although good feelings, new understanding, and blessings will result from your devotional life, your goal is to know and love Him deeply.

EMPHASIS: A Daily Quiet Time is an inspirational period set aside for personal fellowship with God. Discuss the following questions together:

1. *The Purpose of a Devotional Life* —Why is it vital for you to develop a lifestyle of personal fellowship with God?

2. *Good Examples* — Who in scripture or your personal experience most inspires and challenges you by their example of deep devotion toward God?

3. *Personal Prayer* — Consider your prayer and Bible reading; How do they complement one another to produce spiritual blessing?

SUMMARY

God wants you to worship and intimately fellowship with Him. Because He is worthy of your worship, you can seek Him eagerly and expectantly. The examples of godly people in Scripture illustrate the principle of seeking God daily. The Word of God and prayer are the means by which you fellowship with Him. Living by priority and focusing on the right goal will help you maintain your spiritual growth.

LESSON FOUR
PRAYER – EVIDENCE OF DEPENDENCY

4

God created man as a very capable and gifted being. In both mind and spirit, he is unequaled among God's creations. But man was never meant to function on his own, outside of union with God. We were designed to live daily in dependency upon God, and prayer is an important evidence of that dependency.

PROMISES FOR THOSE WHO PRAY

> *"Call to Me, and I will answer you, and I will tell you great and mighty things, which you do not know."* (Jeremiah 33:3)

1. Read Hebrews 4:15 & 16

    What should your attitude be like when you come before God in prayer? *Verse 16* _____

    _____

    Why can you have this attitude? *Verse 15* _____

    _____

    What is available to us at the "throne of grace"? *Verse 16*

    _____

2. What does Matthew 7: 9-11 reveal about God's desire to answer prayer? _____

    _____

    _____

3. Read James 5:16-18

    How was Elijah described? *Verse 17* _____

    _____

    How did God respond to Elijah's prayers? *Verses 17 & 18*

    _____

    _____

    What principle about prayer does the life of Elijah illustrate?

    Verse 16 _____

    _____

4. In 2 Chronicles 7:14, God made a conditional promise. What
    were the...

    Conditions To Be Met

    _____

    _____

    _____

    Promises Given

    _____

    _____

    _____

5. How can anxiety be replaced with God's peace?

    Philippians 4:6 & 7 _____

    _____

"The greatest problem concerning prayer is simply man's
failure to do it. Those who really pray and enjoy this
God-given privilege constitute a very small minority
among the great number of Christians.

"The Christian's greatest resource with God and man is
prayer. With prayer he opens the gates of heaven, enabling God to pour forth His good things upon men." [1]

—E. F. Hallock

Correct the following statement in light of Ephesians 3:20:" God gives you only what you ask for. "

_____

_____

_____

_____

How should this understanding affect your concept of God? _____

_____

_____

_____

How should this affect your prayer life? _____

_____

_____

_____

THOU ART COMING TO A KING

Thou art coming to a King,
Large petitions with thee bring,
For His grace and power are such
None can ever ask too much.
                    —John Newton

CONDITIONS FOR ANSWERED PRAYER

"Until now you have asked for nothing in My name; ask, and you will receive, that your joy may be made full." (John 16:24)

6. The verses below are prayer promises which contain various conditions you must fulfill before God will answer. Look up the verses and write the conditions and promises:

Verse	Conditions	Promises
Matthew 7:7		
Matthew 18:19		
Matthew 21:22		
John 14:13 & 14		
John 15:7		
1 John 5:14 & 15		

7. What hinders answers to prayer?

*Isaiah 59:2*_____

*James 4:2*_____

*James 4:3*_____

✝ *In Mark 11:24, the condition for answered prayer is believing that God has already answered. Meditate on this verse and write out what it reveals about God and prayer:* _____

_____

_____

_____

_____

PERSISTENCY IN PRAYER

"The great fault of the children of God is that they do not continue in prayer; they do not go on praying; they do not persevere." [2]

—George Mueller

8. Jesus told a parable regarding prayer in Luke 18:1-8. What was the major point? *Verse 1*_____

_____

How did the widow apply this? *Verse 5* _____

_____

What is revealed about God in this parable? *Verses 7 & 8*

_____

_____

✝ *Why is persistence in prayer a sign of faith?*

_____

_____

_____

_____

In what way have you demonstrated persistence in prayer?

_____

_____

_____

_____

9. What did the disciples ask Jesus to teach them? *Luke 11:1*

_____

10. Read Luke 11:5-8. In the story Jesus told, why was the request granted? _____

_____

11. Read Mark 10:46-52. What evidence of persistence do you see on the part of Bartimaeus? _____

_____

What were the results of his persistence? _____

_____

Read Matthew 6:7 & 8. What do you think is the difference between "persistence" and "meaningless repetition"? _____

_____

_____

_____

Why would God have you persist in prayer when He already knows your needs? _____

_____

_____

_____

In Matthew 7:7 & 8, the verbs in the Greek language are of *continuous action.* If the verses were written in English to express the clearest meaning, the reading would be, *"Ask and keep on asking, and it shall be given to you; seek and keep on seeking, and you shall find; knock and keep on knocking, and it shall be opened to you. For everyone who asks and keeps on asking keeps on receiving, and he who seeks and keeps on seeking keeps on finding, and to him who knocks and keeps on knocking, it shall be opened."*

LEARNING TO PRAY

"And it came about that while He was praying in a certain place, after He had finished, one of His disciples said to Him, 'Lord, teach us to pray just as John also taught his disciples.'" (Luke 11:1)

12. How are you encouraged to pray?

*Romans 1:9*_____

1 Thessalonians 5:17 _____

"Without ceasing" comes from the Greek word *adialeiptos* which carries the idea of recurring constantly, rather than unbroken continuity. It is a word describing a prayer life which does not miss an opportunity.

13. In God's Word, you are given clear examples to direct your prayer life. Look up the verses in the wheel and write out the request in the appropriate space:

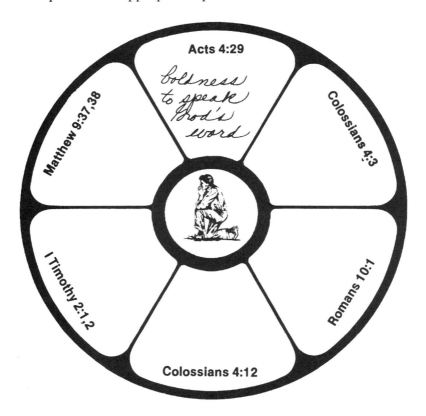

14. Read Colossians 1:9-12. List the things Paul asked the Lord to do for these believers: _____

_____

_____

_____

_____

_____

_____

15. Meditate on Ephesians 6:18. What truths can you learn from this
    verse? _____

    _____

    _____

    _____

16. Why do we often struggle when we try to pray as we should?
    Matthew 26:41 _____

    _____

EMPHASIS: Prayer is the Christian's greatest resource with God
and man. Discuss these questions together:

1. *Promises for Those Who Pray* — How should God's promises
   concerning prayer affect your personal view toward its importance?

2. *Faithfulness in Prayer* —Why is consistency important to the
   development of your prayer life?

3. *Learning to Pray* —How does using a SJ help strengthen your
   prayer life?

SUMMARY

Prayer is an evidence of faith, and God has promised great things for
those who pray. If you are to be effective in prayer, you must meet
God's conditions and be persistent. Praying in every situation and
without missing an opportunity for every need should characterize
your prayer life.

[1] *Always In Prayer*, E.F. Hallock. Published by the author, p. 54.
[2] *George Mueller - Man of Faith*, Edited by A. Sims. Moody Press,
Chicago, p. 12.

LESSON FIVE
SHARING CHRIST WITH OTHERS

5

It is impossible to fathom the depth of love God feels toward His creation or the extent of activity to which God moves to demonstrate His compassion. If Christians were more aware of God's compassion for the lost, two noticeable changes would occur: (1) an increased degree of worship and thanksgiving and (2) an increased concern for the lost, evidenced by more frequent sharing of the good news of salvation.

GOD'S COMPASSION FOR THE LOST

"And he got up and came to his father. But while he was still a long way off, his father saw him, and felt compassion for him, and ran and embraced him, and kissed him... 'For this son of mine was dead and has come to life again!'" (Luke 15:20 - 24)

1. What is God's desire for all people?

    1 Timothy 2:3 & 4 _____

    _____

    _____

    2 Peter 3:9 _____

    _____

2. How are the lost described in Acts 26:18? _____

    _____

3. Read John 3:16. What did God's love for the world cause Him
    to do? _____

    _____

    What might loving the lost cost you? _____

    _____

    _____

    _____

4. What does the word "seek" imply in Luke 19:10? _____

    _____

    _____

5. In Luke 15:3-7, Jesus tells a parable which reveals His compas-
    sion for the lost. Read this parable and list the major points:

    _____

    _____

    _____

    _____

    _____

6. How do the following verses reveal Jesus' compassion for the
    people of Jerusalem?
    Luke 13:34 _____

    _____

    Luke 19:41 & 42 _____

    _____

*How does your attitude toward the lost need to be
changed to become more like Jesus?* _____

_____

_____

_____

_____

OUR PRIVILEGE AND RESPONSIBILITY

"Through Him and for His name's sake, we received grace and apostleship to call people from among all the Gentiles to the obedience that comes from faith."
(Romans 1:5, NIV)

7. How does Paul describe his burden for unbelievers?
    Romans 9:1-3 _____

    _____

    Romans 10:1 _____

    _____

    Why do you think Paul had this burden? _____

    _____

    _____

    _____

8. Read Romans 1:14 & 15
    To whom did Paul feel an obligation? _____

    _____

    _____

    How did he respond to this obligation? _____

    _____

    _____

9. Describe the Italian soldier Cornelius: Acts 10: 2 & 22

    _____

    _____

    _____

    What did Cornelius need? *Acts 11:13 & 14* _____

    _____

✝ *Why do you think the angel didn't tell Cornelius how to be saved?*_____

_____

_____

_____

_____

10. Who has the privilege of sharing Christ with others?

   *2 Corinthians 5:20*_____

SHARING YOUR PERSONAL TESTIMONY

"What we have seen and heard we proclaim to you also, that you also may have fellowship with us; and indeed our fellowship is with the Father, and with His Son Jesus Christ." (1 John 1:3)

11. How did many of the Samaritans come to believe in Jesus?

    *John 4:39*_____

    _____

12. Read Mark 5:19 & 20.

    What did Jesus tell this man to do? *Verse 19*_____

    _____

    _____

    What were the results of his testimony? *Verse 20*_____

    _____

    _____

13. What commission did God give Paul at his conversion?

    *Acts 22:15*_____

    _____

    _____

    _____

14. In giving his testimony, which he often used in witnessing, Paul shared three periods of his life. They are:

Life before becoming a Christian.

Read Acts 22:3-5 and Acts 26:4-11 and briefly describe Paul's life before becoming a Christian: _____

_____

_____

_____

_____

Why and How he became a Christian.

Read Acts 22:7-16 and Acts 26: 12-18 and briefly describe why and how Paul became a Christian:_____

_____

_____

_____

_____

_____

Life after he became a Christian.

Read Acts 9:19-22, Acts 22:21. and Acts 26:19 & 20 and briefly describe Paul's life after becoming a Christian: _____

_____

_____

_____

_____

_____

_____

STEPPING OUT IN FAITH

"For whatever is born of God overcomes the world; and this is the victory that has overcome the world—our faith."
(1 John 5:4)

15. Describe Paul's feelings as he shared the Gospel with the people in Corinth. *1 Corinthians 2:3-5* _____

_____

_____

_____

_____

How was he able to remain faithful to this task? _____

_____

_____

_____

_____

16. What was the reminder given to Timothy regarding fear? *2 Timothy 1:7* _____

_____

_____

17. Peter and John had been warned not to speak in the name of Jesus. What was their response to this threat? *Acts 4:29*

_____

_____

_____

What was the result? *Acts 4:31* _____

_____

_____

_____

18. Read Acts 5:40-42 What happened to some of the early apostles because of their witnessing about Jesus? *Verse 40* _____

_____

What did they do? *Verses 41 & 42* _____

_____

_____

_____

Why do you think these early Christians would witness in the face of such hostility and suffering? _____

_____

_____

_____

Why do you think most Christians today are so reluctant to witness even when they seldom face hostility or suffering? _____

_____

_____

What is needed in our lives to make us more like the early Christians? _____

_____

_____

_____

"I WOULD LIKE TO WITNESS TO HIM, BUT...."

I Don't Know How.

It's Not The Best Time.

I'm Afraid of Failure.

I Don't Have Time.

What Will He Think of Me?

He Doesn't Look Interested.

I'm Ashamed.

With which barrier do you have the greatest struggle?

_____

*What practical step can you take this week to help over-come this barrier?*_____

_____

_____

_____

EMPHASIS: Your personal testimony is a powerful tool for sharing Jesus Christ with others. Discuss the following questions:

1. *God's Compassion for the Lost*—Why should God's great love for sinful men inspire you to tell others about Him?

2. *Our Privilege and Responsibility*—As Christians, what is our obligation to the lost?

3. *Sharing Your Personal Testimony*—Why is your testimony so effective for communicating the gospel to non-Christians?

SUMMARY

God has revealed His deep compassion for the lost and has given His only Son Jesus so that they might return to Him. As Christ's follower, it is both your privilege and your responsibility to share the "good news" of Jesus Christ with non-believers. Giving your personal testimony is an important means of witnessing, and it is one of life's foremost privileges.

LESSON SIX
GOD OUR FATHER

6

Jesus taught His disciples to call God, "Our Father." The Bible teaches that God is all that a father should be to his children. He loves, protects, provides for, and trains them.

THE FATHER'S LOVE

"The LORD appeared to him from afar, saying, 'I have loved you with an everlasting love; Therefore I have drawn you with lovingkindness.'" (Jeremiah 31:3)

1. What was God's motivation in redeeming mankind?
   Ephesians 2:4 & 5 _____

2. How has God shown His love for you? *1 John 3:1* _____
   _____

3. In Luke 15:11-24 Jesus tells a story of a father's love for his son. Read the account and then express in your own words how this illustrates God's love and forgiveness: _____
   _____
   _____
   _____
   _____
   _____

THE FATHER'S PROTECTION

"But the Lord is faithful, and He will strengthen and protect you from the evil one." (2 Thessalonians 3:3)

4. What does God promise in the following verses?

   Psalm 34:7 _____

   _____

   Psalm 125:2 _____

   _____

5. How does Daniel 6:16-23 illustrate the Father's protection of His people? _____

   _____

   _____

   _____

6. What protection does your heavenly Father promise regarding temptations you face? *1 Corinthians 10:13* _____

   _____

   _____

   _____

   _____

   _____

7. What was the Apostle Paul's testimony regarding God's protection? *2 Timothy 4:18* _____

   _____

   _____

   _____

   _____

THE FATHER'S PROVISION

"And my God shall supply all your needs according to His riches in glory in Christ Jesus." (Philippians 4:19)

8. Why can God's children afford not to worry?
    Matthew 6:31 & 32 _____

    _____

    Ephesians 3:20 _____

    _____

9. What assurance of God's provision is found in 1 Peter 5:7?

    _____

    _____

10. What gift has God given that proves He will provide for you?
    Romans 8:32 _____

    _____

    _____

11. What does God want us to do with what He provides?
    1 Timothy 6:17 _____

    _____

    _____

12. Read Psalm 23 and briefly list how God demonstrates both His protection and His provision: _____

    _____

    _____

    _____

    _____

    _____

✝ *Knowing God's protection should eliminate fear and knowing His provision should eliminate worry. What fears or worries do you frequently experience?* _____

_____

_____

_____

*What should you do about your fears and worries?*_____

_____

_____

_____

THE FATHER'S TRAINING

"For those whom the Lord loves He disciplines...God deals with you as with sons; for what son is there whom his father does not discipline?" (Hebrews 12:6 & 7)

13. What should be the goal of each believer? *Ephesians 4:14 & 15*

_____

_____

_____

_____

When one becomes a Christian, he is a spiritual babe. However, he is not to remain a babe, but to grow and mature in Christ.

14. Describe the Christians in 1 Corinthians 3:1-3: _____

_____

_____

_____

15. In Hebrews 5:11-14 the writer states what the believers have become, what they need, and what they ought to be. Read this passage and fill in the chart below:

What They Have Become: _____

What They Need: _____

What They Ought to Be: _____

_____

_____

Describe how you learn to discern between good and evil.

Verse 14 _____

_____

16. Read Hebrews 12:9-11. Why does God discipline us?

Verse 10 _____

_____

Verse 11 _____

_____

17. What means does God use to train His children?

Proverbs 27:17 _____

2 Timothy 3:16 _____

James 1:2-4 _____

What aspect of God's Fatherhood is most meaningful to you? _____

_____

Why? _____

_____

_____

_____

EMPHASIS: We can know our God as Father; this is the blessing of forgiveness and salvation.

Focus on these discussion questions.

1. *The Father's Love*—How can you *know* that God loves you personally?

2. *The Father's Provision*—How can you *know* that God will provide for you in every way?

3. *The Father's Training*—Why is *discipline* a means of training? In what ways has God been training you?

SUMMARY

As a believer, God is your Father. He loves you with an unconditional, forgiving, everlasting love. He has promised to protect you from evil and to give you the power to overcome trials and temptations. He has provided for all your needs in Christ and wants you to enjoy Him and His provisions. He trains you that you might grow and become like Jesus.

LESSON SEVEN
THE MINISTRY OF
THE HOLY SPIRIT

7

God is a Trinity consisting of God the Father, God the Son, and God the Holy Spirit. Who is the Holy Spirit, and what is His role in our lives?

> *"But I (Jesus) tell you the truth, it is to your advantage that I go away; for if I do not go away, the Helper shall not come to you: but if I go, I will send Him to you."* (John 16:7)

HIS MINISTRY BEFORE CONVERSION

1. What is the three-fold ministry of the Holy Spirit to the unbeliever? *John 16:7 & 8* _____

   _____

   _____

2. What is the ministry of the Holy Spirit in John 15:26? _____

   _____

   _____

3. What is the serious consequence of rejecting the Holy Spirit's ministry? *Hebrews 10:29-31* _____

   _____

   _____

   _____

Briefly, how would you summarize the Holy Spirit's ministry to the unbeliever? _____

_____

_____

_____

_____

HIS MINISTRY AT CONVERSION

4. What distinguishes the Christian from the non-Christian?
   Romans 8:9 _____

5. What does the Holy Spirit do for every believer?
   1 Corinthians 12:13 _____

   _____

6. Upon conversion what does every Christian receive?
   1 Corinthians 2:12 _____

Ephesians 1:13 states that at conversion the Holy Spirit "seals" us in Jesus. What do you think this means?

_____

_____

_____

_____

_____

How should this statement affect your security as a believer?

_____

_____

_____

_____

HIS MINISTRY THROUGHOUT YOUR LIFE

Filling

7. Read Galatians 5:16-21.

    What keeps a person from doing what he knows is pleasing to God? *Verses 16 & 17* _____

    _____

    What solution is given by God to overcome the flesh (sinful nature)? *Verses 16 & 17* _____

    _____

What works of the flesh (sinful nature) are hindering you at this point in your life? *Verses 19-21*

_____

_____

_____

_____

8. What two commands are given in Ephesians 5:18?

    (1) _____

    (2) _____

God's way of empowering you to live a victorious Christian life is by filling you with the Holy Spirit, moment-by-moment. You can be filled with (directed and empowered by), the Holy Spirit if you:

(1) Live by faith.

> *"I have been crucified with Christ; and it is no longer I who live, but Christ lives in me; and the life which I now live in the flesh I live by faith in the Son of God, who loved me, and delivered Himself up for me."* (Galatians 2:20) *"And without faith it is impossible to please Him."* (Hebrews 11:6a)

(2) Confess and turn away from all known sin.
   "If we confess our sins, He is faithful and righteous to forgive us our sins and to cleanse us from all unrighteousness." (1 John 1:9)

(3) Yield every area of your life to Christ.
   "For all who are being led by the Spirit of God, these are the sons of God." (Romans 8:14)

9. Read Ephesians 3:14-19 and answer the following questions: What is one of the Holy Spirit's roles in your life? *Verse 16*

_____

_____

_____

What is the result? *Verses 17-19* _____

_____

_____

_____

_____

_____

_____

10. Peter and John were arrested and threatened for preaching about Jesus. Read Acts 4:23-31 and answer the following questions: What did they need? *Verses 29 & 30* _____

_____

What did they do? *Verse 31* _____

_____

_____

_____

What happened? *Verse 31* _____

_____

_____

_____

_____

✝ *How did God meet their need?* _____

_____

_____

_____

When you daily realize personal needs, what should you do?

_____

_____

_____

_____

Perfecting

11. What work does the Holy Spirit do in the believer's life?

    1 Peter 1:2 _____

    What does this work enable us to do? _____

    _____

    Sanctify means to *cleanse, purify,* and *set apart for special use.*

12. Why is it important to respond to the purifying work of the Holy Spirit? *2 Timothy 2:20-22* _____

    _____

    _____

13. What does the Holy Spirit use to perfect believers?

Romans 5:3-5 _____

Ephesians 6:17 _____

14. How is the perfecting ministry of the Holy Spirit described in 2 Corinthians 3:18? _____

_____

_____

Empowering

15. What effect will the Holy Spirit have upon believers' lives?

Acts 1:8 _____

16. Read Ephesians 4:25-30.

What warnings are given regarding a believer's relationship with the Holy Spirit?

Verse 30 _____

_____

Read the following verses and list things that grieve the Holy Spirit:

Verse 25 _____

Verse 26 _____

Verse 27 _____

Verse 28 _____

Verse 29 _____

17. Read 1 Thessalonians 5:16-19.

What additional warning is given to the Christian about his relationship to the Holy Spirit?

Verse 19 _____

_____

_____

In your own words define:

Grieving the Spirit _____

_____

_____

_____

_____

Quenching the Spirit _____

_____

_____

_____

God's people need power to witness. An equally important need is the power to live a Christ-like life on a daily basis.

18. How is the fullness of the Holy Spirit demonstrated in the Christian's life? *Galatians 5:22 & 23* _____

_____

_____

EMPHASIS: The Holy Spirit's ministry empowers us to live a life that is pleasing to God. Discuss these questions together:

1. *His Ministry Before Your Conversion* —What did the Holy Spirit do in your life before you came to know Jesus?

2. *His Ministry at Conversion* —Where was He *at* the time of your conversion experience?

3. *His Ministry Throughout Your Life* — Discuss His ministry of filling, perfecting, and empowering. What *evidence* of His activity do you now enjoy?

SUMMARY

The Holy Spirit is God at work in the world today. His ministry to people begins before conversion by bearing witness of Jesus and bringing conviction of sin. At conversion He comes to dwell in each believer and places that believer into the body of Christ. For the rest of the believer's life, He ministers by filling each one who submits himself and his needs to God, perfecting the believer to "become like Jesus." He leads, protects, and empowers the Christian to live a victorious Christian life!

LESSON EIGHT
THE IMPORTANCE
OF GOD'S WORD

8

The Bible is not just another book of religious instruction written by holy men. The Bible is God's authoritative Word to you. It is a book about life and how He wants you to live it.

THE AUTHORITY OF THE SCRIPTURES

> *"But He answered and said, 'It is written, "Man shall not live on bread alone, but on every Word that proceeds out of the mouth of God.'"* (Matthew 4:4)

1. Who wrote the Scriptures? *2 Peter 1:20 & 21* _____

   _____

   What do you think the phrase "moved (carried along) by the Holy Spirit" means?_____

   _____

   _____

2. Peter included Paul's letters with what other writings?
   2 Peter 3:15 & 16 _____
   What authority does this imply for Paul's letters?_____

   _____

   _____

3. What does 2 Timothy 3:16 indicate about the inspiration of the
    Scriptures?_____

    _____

    _____

> The Greek word for *inspired* is *theopneustos* which
> literally means *God-breathed.*

4. What do the following verses indicate about Jesus' view of the
    authority of Scripture? *John 10:34 & 35*_____

    _____

5. What sometimes undermines the authority of the Word of God?
    Mark 7:9 _____

    _____

> *If God and His Word are not the ultimate authority in
> a person's life, what is?*_____
>
> _____
>
> _____
>
> _____
>
> _____

HOW GOD'S WORD CAME TO US

Used by Permission [1]

THE RELIABILITY OF THE SCRIPTURES

Are the scriptures reliable? Can you be certain that the Bible is God's Word? After many centuries and many translations, can you be sure this is what God said?

6. What did Jesus say about the Word of God? *John 17:17*_____

    _____

    _____

7. What do you learn about God's Word from the following verses?

    Isaiah 40:8 _____

    _____

    *Mark 13:31*_____

    _____

    1 Peter 1:24 & 25 _____

    _____

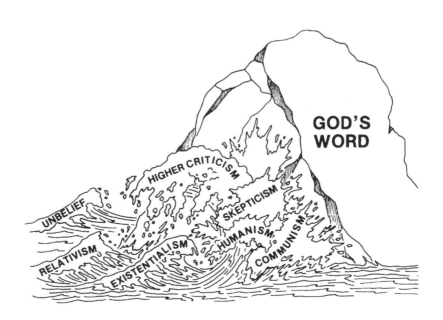

THE RELIABILITY OF THE BIBLICAL DOCUMENTS

The Bible was written over a sixteen-hundred-year period by 34 to 40 different writers in twelve different countries. Though it is composed of 66 different books written in three different languages, there is a profound unity of its teachings and message. Modern scholarship and archaeology have examined manuscripts and Biblical records. The findings substantiate the reliability of the Bible.

The Old Testament is composed of 39 books. For many years the oldest known manuscripts in existence were dated at 900 A.D. These manuscripts were the product of a group of Jewish scribes known as Massoretes. How could one know whether the Massoretic Text was pure or whether it had been contaminated by time and multiple transmissions? If a manuscript much older could be found, the comparison of the two would prove the validity of the Massoretic Text.

In 1947, in the caves around the Dead Sea, ancient scrolls were discovered which contained Isaiah 38-66 in thousands of fragments. These Dead Sea Scrolls were dated at 150-70 B.C. That is a text 1,000 years older than any other known Old Testament manuscript. A comparison of the Massoretic Text with the Dead Sea Scrolls showed very insignificant variance in the text, primarily spelling and word choice.

Scholar R. Laird Harris concluded, "We can be sure that copyists worked with great care and accuracy on the Old Testament, even back to 225 B.C. Indeed, it would be rash skepticism that would now deny we have our Old Testament in a form very close to that used by Ezra when he taught the Law to those who had returned from Babylonian captivity." [2]   The Old Testament is reliable, and its message of the coming Messiah is clear.

The New Testament, composed of 27 books, was written in Greek and was substantially complete about 100 A.D. [3] About 4,000 Greek manuscripts, in whole or in part, are in existence. [4] One of the oldest fragments, John 18:31-33, was discovered in Egypt and dated at about 130 A.D. This is not more than 40 years after the original composition.

Regarding the New Testament text, Sir Fredric Kenyon says, "The interval, then, between the dates of the original composition and the earliest extant evidence becomes so small as to be in fact negligible, and the last foundation for any doubt that the Scriptures have come down to us substantially as they were written has now been removed. Both the authenticity and the general integrity of the books of the New Testament may be regarded as finally established." [5] The New Testament is reliable. No other book of antiquity has as many manuscripts or evidence of validity as the New Testament.

> Modern scholarship has been a friend of the truth. You are studying a Bible which can be trusted. It is God's inspired Word.

8.   What does Numbers 23:19 say about God's keeping His Word?

_____

_____

✝ *What is the relationship between the reliability of*
Scripture and the trustworthiness of God? _____

_____

_____

_____

_____

_____

_____

_____

GOD'S WORD

I paused last eve beside the blacksmith's door,
  And heard the anvil ring, the vesper's chime,
And looking in I saw upon the floor
  Old hammers, worn with beating years of time.

"How many anvils have you had," said I,
  "To wear and batter all these hammers so?"
"Just one," he answered. Then with twinkling eye,
  "The anvil wears the hammers out, you know."

And so, I thought, the anvil of God's Word
  For ages skeptics' blows have beat upon,
But though the noise of falling blows was heard
  The anvil is unchanged, the hammers gone.

—John Clifford

THE SUFFIENCY OF THE SCRIPTURES

*"All Scripture is inspired by God and profitable for teach-
ing, for reproof, for correction, for training in righteousness; that the man of God may be adequate, equipped for
every good work."* (2 Timothy 3:16 & 17)

9. God through His Word meets the needs in the lives of people.
    Look up the verses below and fill in the appropriate blank:

Psalm 37:31	John 15:3
Psalm 119:105	1 Corinthians 10:11
John 5:39 & 40	1 Timothy 4:6
John 8:32	2 Timothy 3:15

Hebrews 4:12

Functions of the Word	Verse
Discerns motives	
Leads people to salvation	
Testifies of Jesus Christ	
Gives stability to your walk	
Sets people free	
Nourishes	
Instructs	
Guides	
Cleanses	

✝ *How does the Word of God minister to you?* _____

_____

_____

_____

_____

_____

10. Read Psalm 119:97-100. What happens when a person truly meditates on God's Word? _____

_____

_____

_____

How important is the Word of God to you? _____

_____

_____

If someone observed your daily schedule, how important would he conclude the Word of God is to you? _____

_____

_____

_____

THE INDISPENSABILITY OF THE SCRIPTURES

"...I have treasured the words of His mouth more than my necessary food." (Job 23:12)

11. What is the value of the Scriptures in the following verses?
Jeremiah 15:16 _____
What is meant by "eat them"? _____

_____

Acts 20:32 _____

_____

What is meant by "build you up"? _____

_____

_____

1 Peter 2:2 _____
What is meant by "grow"? _____

_____

12.   The Bible speaks of a process by which a man becomes prosperous and successful. Read Joshua 1:8 and complete the steps in the process below:

SUCCESS

3.

2.

1. Intake of the Word—*"not depart out of your mouth"*

13. What process is involved in maintaining a pure life?
Psalm 119:9-11 _____

_____

_____

14. Read Luke 10:38-42
What was Mary doing? *Verse 39* _____

_____

How did Jesus evaluate Mary's actions? *Verse 42* _____

_____

What kept Martha from spending quality time with Jesus?
Verses 40 & 41 _____

_____

_____

What hindrances tend to keep you from spending time with the Lord in His Word? _____

_____

_____

_____

_____

15. In the space provided below, write out your plan for making the Word of God an important part of your life: _____

_____

_____

_____

_____

_____

_____

"The vigor of our spiritual life will be in exact proportion to the place held by the Bible in our life and thoughts. I solemnly state this from the experience of fifty-four years." [6]

George Mueller

EMPHASIS: The Bible is God's Word; it focuses on life and how He wants you to live it. Discuss these questions together:

1. *The Reliability of Scripture*—How can you be certain that the Bible is God's Word? (Note the illustration on page 209 and the discussion on the Biblical documents on pages 211 & 212.)

2. *The Sufficiency of Scripture*—How is God's Word meeting the specific needs in your life?

3. *The Indispensability of Scripture*—Explain why the Bible is our sole authority for spiritual life.

SUMMARY

The Bible is the authoritative, "God-breathed" Word of God to man. The text is historically reliable and has been preserved throughout the centuries. It is sufficient to equip you to live a successful life. It is the indispensable source of knowing God and His plan for your life.

[1] *Theographics*, Illustration by Harold Bullock and Milt Hughes.

[2] *How Reliable is the Old Testament Text? Can I Trust My Bible?*, R. Laird Harris, Moody Press, pp. 124, 130. © 1963, Used by permission.

[3] *New Testament Documents: Are They Reliable?*, F.F. Bruce. Wm. B. Eerdmans, p. 12. © 1948. Used by permission.

[4] Ibid, Bruce, p. 16.

[5] *The Bible and Archaeology*, Sir Fredric Kenyon. Harper and Row, pp. 288ff. © 1940. Used by permission.

[6] *Halley's Bible Handbook*, p.4. © 1965. Used by permission.

LESSON NINE
THE CHURCH – A
SUPPORTIVE FELLOWSHIP

9

The primary mission of the church appears to be threefold:

To *evangelize* the lost.
To *establish* the converts.
To *equip* the disciples *in order to serve.*

As these three distinctive but overlapping ministries are occurring, the church accomplishes its God-given calling.

THE MISSION OF THE CHURCH

"The task is never complete until the evangelized becomes the evangeliser."

EVANGELIZING

"So the church throughout all Judea and Galilee and Samaria enjoyed peace, being built up; and, going on in the fear of the Lord and in the comfort of the Holy Spirit, it continued to increase." (Acts 9:31)

1. What is the mission Jesus gave to His church?
   Matthew 28:19 & 20 _____

   _____

   _____

Acts 1:8 _____

2. What was one dominant characteristic of the young churches?

    Acts 8:4 _____

    Colossians 1:5 & 6 _____

    _____

    1 Thessalonians 1:8 _____

    _____

✝ *If everyone in my church were evangelizing as I am, what would be the impact of my church on the lost?*

_____

_____

_____

_____

ESTABLISHING

3. How were the young Christians established...

    at Antioch? *Acts 11:23 & 26* _____

    _____

    in Asia Minor? *Acts 14:21 & 22* _____

    _____

    at Corinth? *Acts 18:11* _____

    _____

4. Upon believing in Jesus, what did the early Christians do?

    Acts 2:41 _____

    Acts 8:12 _____

5. In order to establish the young believers in Colossae, what did Paul exhort them to do? *Colossians 2:6 & 7* _____

    _____

    _____

✝ *What are the essential ingredients in becoming estab-*
lished in your faith in Christ? _____

_____

_____

_____

What is helping you most as you seek to become estab-
lished in your faith? _____

_____

_____

_____

_____

EQUIPPING

6. Ephesians 4:11-16 speaks of the equipping ministry of the
    church.

    Who are the equippers? *Verse 11* _____

    _____

    _____

    What are you being equipped to do? *Verse 12* _____

    _____

    _____

    What are the characteristics of the members of such a church?
    Verses 13, 16 _____

    _____

    _____

    _____

    _____

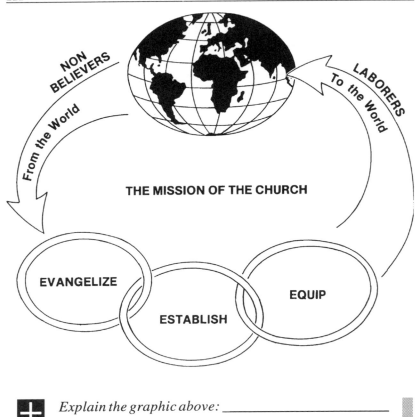

NON BELIEVERS
From the World

LABORERS
To the World

THE MISSION OF THE CHURCH

EVANGELIZE

ESTABLISH

EQUIP

Explain the graphic above: _____

_____

_____

_____

_____

_____

_____

SERVING

7. To whom are Christians to minister?

    Galatians 6:10 _____

_____

8. How did the following people carry out their ministries?

Phillip, *Acts 8:5* _____

Dorcus, *Acts 9:36-39* _____

_____

Paul, *Acts 18:23* _____

_____

Samaritan, *Luke 10:30-37* _____

_____

> *Read James 2:15-17 and explain this statement, "faith without works is dead":* _____
>
> _____
>
> _____
>
> _____
>
> _____

STRUCTURE OF THE CHURCH

"For even as the body is one and yet has many members, and all the members of the body, though they are many, are one body, so also is Christ." (1 Corinthians 12:12)

9. What is Christ's position in the church? *Colossians 1:18*

_____

_____

10. Read Romans 12:4-6

To what is the church compared? *Verse 4* _____

_____

What makes each member of the church unique? *Verse 6*

_____

11. Read 1 Corinthians 12:14-20. Why is each member of the Lord's body important? _____

_____

_____

_____

12. How is the body of Christ built up? *Ephesians 4:15 & 16*

_____

_____

_____

13. Why did God give gifted leaders to the church?

Ephesians 4:11 & 12 _____

_____

_____

In the early church, certain offices or roles emerged. The people who assumed these offices had to meet spiritual qualifications. Acquaint yourself with these qualifications by reading the passages below:

Office		Qualifications
Pastor Elder Bishop } used synonymously		Titus 1:5-9 1 Timothy 3:1-7
Deacons		1 Timothy 3:8-12

14. What attitude should each member of the body have toward the leaders? 1 Thessalonians 5:12 & 13 _____

_____

_____

FUNCTION OF THE CHURCH

The function of a church is the combined function of each individual church member. Only as individual members of the church assume personal accountability to God and obedience to Scripture does the church as a body fulfill its mission.

15. What testimony will a unified church have to non-believers? *John 17:21, 23* _____

_____

_____

16. Acts 2:42 lists the activities of the first New Testament church. List the four activities and the purpose of the activity today:

Church Activity	**Purpose of Activity**
_____	_____
_____	_____
_____	_____
_____	_____

17. What was the purpose of fellowship in Hebrews 10:24 & 25?

_____

_____

In your church, has fellowship with other believers helped accomplish this in your life? _____

Explain: _____

_____

_____

_____

18. What did the early Christians do?

    Acts 8:4, 35 _____

    _____

19. How was the church to deal with those in the congregation who
    refused to repent from sin? *Matthew 18:15-17* _____

    _____

    _____

    _____

WARFARE OF THE CHURCH

*"...upon this rock I will build My church; and the gates of
Hades shall not overpower it."* (Matthew 16:18)

20. Who is the prime enemy of the church? *Ephesians 6:11-13*

    _____

21. What was the faulty thinking in Peter's life that Jesus attributed
    to Satan? *Matthew 16:23* _____

    _____

22. The early church was a growing, dynamic fellowship of believ-
    ers and yet it had several problems. Match the following Scrip-
    tures with the corresponding answer:

Acts 5:3 & 4	False teachers
Acts 6:1, 3	Immorality
Romans 14:3	Quarreling
1 Corinthians 1:11 & 12	Poor organization
1 Corinthians 5:1	Judging one another
Galatians 1:6 & 7	Lying—Dishonesty

23. In the Corinthian church, what were some of the internal con-
    flicts? *1 Corinthians 3:1-3* _____

    _____

    _____

24. What were some opposing forces to the first century church?

   Acts 4:15-20 _____

   _____

   Acts 8:1 _____

   _____

   Colossians 2:8 _____

   _____

   1 John 2:18 & 19 _____

   _____

25. In spite of its internal and external problems, what did the first century church accomplish?

   Romans 1:8 _____

   _____

   Colossians 1:6 _____

   _____

Why do you think the first century church was able to overcome its problems? _____

_____

_____

_____

_____

What application does this have for today? _____

_____

_____

_____

_____

EMPHASIS: The local church has been designed by God to encourage and equip you for your ministry in the world. Discuss the following questions:

1. *The Mission of the Church*—How would you describe the mission of your church in your community?

2. *The Function of the Church*—How does your personal obedience and lifestyle relate to the proper functioning of the church?

3. *The Warfare of the Church*—Who or what are the enemies of the Christian message in your experience, and what are you doing about it?

SUMMARY

The mission of the church is to evangelize the lost, establish the converts, and equip the disciples for service to both Christians and non-Christians. The church structure is likened to a body, with Christ as the head and all the members as equal and important parts. God has given leaders to the church and equipped each member with a special gift that the body might be built up. As the church functions in the world, the world is influenced toward Christ. Satan and carnality are the enemies of the church and create disunity and disharmony, but these challenges will not keep the church from accomplishing its God-given mission!

"And this Gospel of the kingdom shall be preached in the whole world for a witness to all the nations, and then the end shall come." (Matthew 24:14)

APPENDICES

APPENDIX A
QUIET TIME
READING
GUIDE

"Thy word is a lamp to my feet, and a light to my path."
(Psalm 119:105)

Review Page 6 in your SJ before you begin. Read the scriptures with personal application in mind. As you read each morning, come before the Lord with these prayerful attitudes:

Petition: Lord, help me to . . .

Adoration: Lord, You are . . .

Thanksgiving: Lord, I thank You so much for . . .

Confession: Lord, please forgive me for . . .

Use the notetaking section of your SJ to record any questions about passages which you find difficult to understand during your daily Quiet Times. Ask your Discipler to answer these questions during your sessions together. Start by reading Ephesians 1:1-14 during your first daily Quiet Time. Continue reading successive passages. You may wish to break these reading segments into smaller portions by stopping at each new scriptural insight which you find. Because it normally takes thirteen weeks to complete these ten sessions, we have included 100 suggested Quiet Time readings.

Ephesians

1:1 - 14
1:15 - 23
2:1 - 10
2:11 - 22
3:1 - 13
3:14 - 21
4:1 - 16
4:17 - 32
5:1 - 21
5:22 - 33
6:1 - 9
6:10 - 24

Philippians

1:1 - 11
1:12 - 30
2:1 - 18
2:19 - 30
3:1 - 11
3:12 - 21
4:1 - 9
4:10 - 23

Colossians

1:1 - 14
1:15 - 23
1:24 - 29
2:1 - 12
2:13 - 23
3:1 - 17
3:18 - 25
4:1 - 6
4:7 - 18

1 Thessalonians

1:1 - 10
2:1 - 12
2:13 - 20
3: 1 - 13
4:1 - 12
4:13 - 18
5:1 - 11
5:12 - 28

2 Thessalonians

1:1 - 12
2:1 - 12
2:13 - 17
3:1 - 15
3:16 - 18

1 Timothy

1:1 - 11
1:12 - 20
2: 1 - 15
3:1 - 16
4:1 - 16
5:1 - 10
5:11 - 25
6:1 - 10
6:11 - 21

2 Timothy

1:1 - 18
2:1 - 13
2:14 - 26
3:1 - 9
3:10 - 17
4:1 - 8
4:9 -22

Titus
1:1 - 16
2:1 - 15
3:1 - 15

Philemon
1:1 - 25

James
1: 1 - 18
1:19 - 27
2:1 - 13
2:14 - 26
3:1 - 12
3:13 - 18
4:1 - 12
4:13 - 17
5:1 - 12
5:13 - 20

1 Peter
1:1 - 12
1:13 - 25
2:1 - 12
2:13 - 25
3:1 - 7
3:8 - 22
4:1 - 11
4:12 - 19
5:1 - 14

2 Peter
1:1 - 11
1:12 - 21
2:1 - 12
2:13 - 22
3:1 - 18

1 John
1:1 - 10
2:1 - 14
2:15 - 29
3:1 - 10
3:11 - 24
4:1 - 6
4:7 - 21
5:1 - 12
5:13 - 21

2 John
1:1 - 13

3 John
1:1 - 14

Jude
1:1 - 16
1:17 - 25

After you have completed these Quiet Time reading segments, you can enjoy reading the rest of the New Testament using the schedule on page 88 of your SJ. Start in Matthew.

"And let us not lose heart in doing good, for in due time we shall reap if we do not grow weary." (Galatians 6:9)

APPENDIX B
SCRIPTURE
MEMORY

"And these words, which I am commanding you today, shall be on your heart; and you shall teach them diligently to your sons and shall talk of them when you sit in your house and when you walk by the way and when you lie down and when you rise up."
(Deuteronomy 6:6 & 7)

From the earliest days of our faith, long before Bibles could be printed, we were commanded to hide God's Word in our hearts. It was to be the center of our family life and a vital part of every day's experience.

Jesus is our best example for scripture memory (Matthew 4:1-11). All through His ministry He demonstrated His great familiarity with Scripture. He made over 60 specific references to the Old Testament in the four gospels.

Merely learning to say a verse is not a worthy spiritual objective. The goal is to *live with* a memory verse until it saturates your mind and affects the way you think and act.

WHY MEMORIZE SCRIPTURE?

Scripture Memory will:

1. Encourage you to grow in Christ's likeness – The more Scripture you commit to memory, the easier it will be for the Holy

Spirit to guide and protect you throughout your life. *"I will instruct you and teach you in the way you should go; I will guide you with My eye."* (Psalm 32:8, NKJV)

2. Help you overcome worry by knowing God's promises – *"Be anxious for nothing, but in everything by prayer and supplication with thanksgiving let your requests be made known to God."* (Philippians 4:6)

3. Direct you to resist temptation and live in purity – *"Thy Word I have treasured in my heart, that I might not sin against Thee."* (Psalm 119:11)

4. Remind You of the consequences of sin – *"Do not be deceived: God cannot be mocked. A man reaps what he sows."* (Galatians 6:7, NIV)

5. Equip you to confidently share Christ with others – *"Always be prepared to give an answer to everyone who asks you to give the reason for the hope that you have."* (1 Peter 3:15, NIV)

6. Channel your thoughts in a positive direction – *"Let your eyes look directly ahead, and let your gaze be fixed straight in front of you."* (Proverbs 4:25)

7. Give you direction for daily decisions – *"Thy Word is a lamp unto my feet and a light unto my path."* (Psalm 119:105)

8. Help you be consistent and diligent, even through difficult trials. – *"Consider it pure joy, my brothers, when you face trials of many kinds, because you know that the testing of your faith develops perseverance. Perseverance must finish its work so that you may be mature and complete, not lacking anything."* (James 1:2-4, NIV)

9. Maintain a pure thought life – *"Finally, brethren, whatever is true, whatever is honorable, whatever is right, whatever is pure, whatever is lovely, whatever is of good repute, if there is any*

excellence and if anything worthy of praise, let your mind dwell on these things." (Philippians 4:8)

HELPFUL HINTS FOR MEMORIZING SCRIPTURE

1. Use a *memory packet* or *booklet*, and always *keep* it with you. (See Resource Section, page 257).

2. Review memory verses after prayer at *every* meal.

3. Repeat the reference *before* and *after* each verse.

4. Prayerfully *apply* each verse to your daily life.

5. Be consistent – *"Discipline yourself for the purpose of Godliness."* (1 Timothy 4:7)

6. Always seek to learn your verses perfectly. This will improve your retention and give you greater confidence when quoting Scripture.

7. Learn the *context* of the verse. Read the verses immediately before and after the verse in your Bible. Through this practice, you will gain a more accurate understanding of the Scripture.

8. Repeat portions of the verse *aloud* as you memorize.

9. Concentrate on a few *key words* until a phrase is completely memorized. Add additional phrases one at a time until you have memorized the entire verse.

10. Use only *one* translation for memorization.

11. Memorize scripture with a friend and encourage each other – to *live* what you learn! *"I will meditate on Thy precepts, and regard Thy ways. I shall delight in Thy statutes; I shall not forget Thy word."* (Psalm 119:15-16)

APPENDIX C
CHRISTIAN
MEDITATION

C

*"I will meditate on Thy precepts, and regard Thy ways. I shall
delight in Thy statutes; I shall not forget Thy Word."*
(Psalm 119:15 & 16)

Christian meditation involves prayerfully considering, reflecting
and focusing on all the aspects of a truth, then seeking to apply that
truth to your life. True meditation leads to godly thoughts and
actions!

In 2 Timothy 2:7 (Amplified), Paul tells Timothy to meditate on the
Scriptural truths that he is sharing with him." *Consider, reflect,
think about, ponder these things I am saying (the Scriptures) –
understand them and grasp their application – for the Lord will
grant you full insight and understanding into all this."*

Let's look at an example of how you would meditate upon a verse.
Romans 15:13 states, *"Now may the God of hope fill you with all joy
and peace in believing, that you may abound in hope by the power
of the Holy Spirit."* Slowly read the verse several times and consider
what God wants to say to you personally. (Sample prayer) "Lord, I
am open to any truth that you want to teach me." Prayerfully focus
on a key word like "hope." "You are truly a God of hope. Without
You, there is no hope. No matter what my negative circumstances
may be, I can always find hope in You as I learn to trust in You."

Non-verbal thought is a form of prayer. Let's assume that your thoughts continue on this theme. "Because I am Your child, I have the confident expectation that You are accomplishing Your will in and through me. You love me and care about every detail of my life. You are not only a God of hope, but You give me something that no one else can give. You provide a supernatural joy and peace! You not only give me encouragement; You enable me to *abound* in hope! There is never a reason for me to ever be hopeless, because I am Your child. You are the source of all hope. I don't have to work it up, it is mine *by the power of Your Holy Spirit who lives in me.*"

APPENDIX D
SPIRITUAL
OVERFLOW

"Discipline yourself for the purpose of godliness."
(1 Timothy 4:7)

Evangelism
Fruit of the Spirit

Matthew 28:18-20

Evangelism
Fruit of the Spirit

Genuine love for God and man
resulting in a natural obedience
to go and make disciples in the power
of the Holy Spirit

Godly character & personal purity

Meditating on the Word

Memorizing Scripture

Daily Bible Study/Topical Reading

Daily Quiet Time

Hear the Word–Taking notes

Reliance on the Holy Spirit
for the empowerment to
accomplish His tasks

Decision to grow spiritually
and yield to God's word

New Believer with Assurance

CHRIST
1 Corinthians 3:11

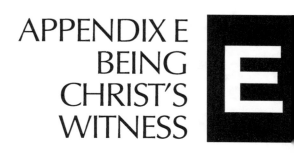

APPENDIX E
BEING
CHRIST'S
WITNESS

"But you shall receive power when the Holy Spirit has come upon you; and you shall be My witnesses both in Jerusalem, and in all Judea and Samaria, and even to the remotest part of the earth."
(Acts 1:8)

Spiritual gifts are special God-given empowerments given to Christians to carry out certain ministries for the common good of the body.

ILLUSTRATION: Once a church member was invited to go witnessing with an outreach group. He said he didn't witness because he didn't have the *gift* of evangelism. This raised the question, "who should share his faith; all Christians or just those who have a special gift?"

1. **Matthew 28:18** & **19** says, *"All authority has been given to Me in heaven and on earth. Go therefore and make disciples of all the nations, baptizing them in the name of the Father and the Son and the Holy Spirit, teaching them to observe all that I have commanded you; and lo, I am with you always; even to the end of the age."* When Jesus gave this commission to the church, He didn't say, ". . . those of you with the gift of evangelism go make disciples. . ." The commission was given to all Christians for all time. It is as much our privilege to make disciples today, as it was for the first century believers.

2. Did God ever say, "You don't need to live by faith unless you have the gift of faith? You don't need to serve unless you have the gift of service? You don't need to be merciful unless you have the gift of mercy? You don't need to tithe unless you have the gift of giving?" No, even though not everyone is called to be an evangelist, we are *all* called to share our witness with others (Acts 1:8).

3. What are the functions of a person with the ministry of evangelism; an evangelist? You would naturally expect a person with this calling to be involved in sharing the good news with others!

    In Ephesians 4:11 & 12 we read, *"And He gave some as apostles, and some as prophets, and some as evangelists, and some as pastors and teachers, for the equipping of the saints for the work of service."* The evangelist is given to the church not only to preach, but to help equip the saints for their ministry. What would an evangelist equip the saints to do? To *teach* and *train* them in how to effectively share the gospel. Do you see why God's wisdom is far superior to our own? How much more efficient it is for an evangelist to teach and train hundreds, even thousands of people to witness, as compared with the evangelist spreading the good news by himself.

    The spiritual office and calling of an evangelist is as specific and unique as that of the pastor or missionary, but all of us are called and potentially empowered to be effective personal witnesses.

"For I am confident of this very thing, that He who began a good work in you will perfect it until the day of Christ Jesus."
(Philippians 1:6)

APPENDIX F
A BIBLE
STUDY
METHOD

F

". . .If you abide in My word, then you are truly disciples of Mine."
(John 8:31)

A good friend of mine says, "A Quiet Time keeps your ship afloat, but Bible Study puts wind in your sails." I couldn't agree with him more. There is no way to over stress the importance of daily Bible study. So far, you have both been using the LCD. This is a tool specifically designed to teach basic Christian doctrine, but in four more sessions you will have finished this study. It is important that you now plan ahead to enjoy your own independent Bible Study.

Sometimes we forget what a privilege it is to have the printed word so readily available. If a 1st century Christian wanted to learn more about God's Word, he would sometimes have to travel for miles to hear a teacher. He could only listen when the teacher was available. In contrast, we now have daily access to the greatest Bible teachers in the world. Good books and commentaries can bring them right into your living room as often and as long as you want. It's surprising that more Christians do not take advantage of this tremendous privilege.

Have you ever wondered why Christians young and old come back from camps and retreats so motivated to serve the Lord? The answer is that they have been *focusing on the Lord and spending time in His teachings.* It requires discipline to stay on the cutting edge of

Christian growth. All to often, we come home and get back into the rut of spending time with God only on Sundays. Eventually, we settle into a mediocre spiritual lifestyle. We seem surprised when this happens over and over again. Some people feel that getting "super-charged" during a retreat or a revival meeting should last them for several months of effective ministry. Like fad dieting, this approach to growth only leads to a cycle of joy followed by discouragement.

You don't have to settle for a mediocre life! The key is consistent daily intake from God's Word and a heart that is eager for personal spiritual growth. Soon you will be used by Him and then the fulfillment will begin.

There is no greater joy than knowing that you are growing spiritually and that you are also being used to minister to others. Ask yourself these honest questions: "Do I really want to grow, or am I willing to be a nominal, defeated Christian? Do I really want to impact my world for Christ, or am I content to sit back and watch the world become increasingly dysfunctional and spiritually indifferent?" If you commit yourself to grow in Christ, you will have to decide to study the Bible.

When Jesus was on earth, everyone crowded around Him because they wanted His time and attention. Why did they want to be with Him? Because they knew that through Him they would be *changed*!

Eleven ordinary men were transformed into leaders and they shook the world for Christ. Their secret was spending quality time with the Master. Why should it be any different for us today? Anyone who spends quality time with Christ studying His Word will never be the same. The more time spent studying and applying His teachings, the more you will become like Him. *"Now as they observed the confidence of Peter and John, and understood that they were uneducated and untrained men, they were marveling, and began to recognize them as having been with Jesus."* (Acts 4:13) Spending time with the Lord made the difference for Peter and John.

The following Bible study method is simple, inexpensive, and inspirational – it can be enjoyed for months and years. It can take you completely through the Old and New Testaments. Wouldn't it be wonderful to make a serious commitment to study the entire Bible?

LET'S GET STARTED!

Preparation Steps:

First – Use an up to date translation of the Bible.

Second – You will need to use a Bible that has blank areas in the margins. Wide margin Bibles are listed in the Resource Section, (page 257). These Bibles give ample space to record insights in the margins. You may wish to use a simple notebook to record insights.

Third – You will want the best Bible teachers available in print. We suggest that you begin with the *Be* series from Scripture Press Publications. It will take you completely through the New Testament and into the Old Testament. Start with Matthew. In the *Be* series, this book is entitled *Be Loyal*, and is written by Dr. Warren Wiersbe. (See Resource Section, page 257). With over 3 million copies of this series in print, we have found it to be an excellent source for sound Biblical teaching.

Fourth – After you have obtained your tools, decide on a specific time each day to study the Bible. If you say to yourself, "I will study the Bible when I have extra time," you probably won't do it. Bible study cannot be viewed as an *optional* discipline. You must realize that it is a *necessity* for your spiritual growth. Your perception of its importance will determine how often you study the Bible. Example: When you decide on a specific time each night, the clock helps remind you of your commitment. Somehow, you never have time for things unless you specifically plan to do them! It is helpful to place your Bible and study tools in a place where they are easily visible. Spending 30 - 60 minutes in Bible study each night is a good way to start. Example: If you have children, plan to study after the kids are asleep. Be practical and plan for long term success.

Bible Study Steps:

First – Begin by having prayer and telling the Lord that you are open and ready to obey any truth that He shows you. Tell Him that you want to be a Godly man or woman. Ask Him to show you truths and insights that will help you grow spiritually.

Second – Begin by reading the first chapter of Matthew in your Bible.

Third – Next, open the *Be Loyal* book and read the teaching about Matthew Chapter 1. As you read, ask the Lord to make you aware of Biblical truths and insights that you can apply to your own life. As the Lord gives you understanding and insights, write them in the margin of your Bible or notebook next to the verse.

Fourth – Slowly read through the chapter verse by verse again and carefully consider the meaning of each passage. As you read, pray that the Holy Spirit will reveal insights and truths that your Bible teacher may have missed. The Lord will often give you additional truths. Write these insights in the margins of your Bible or in your Bible study notebook.

Chapter 1 of Matthew is now lined with pearls of Biblical truth and insights. It is tempting to stop – one step short of application. The Bible starts making a difference in our lives when we apply it personally.

Fifth – The last step is application. We must be ready to *yield* and *obey* His will. This step is where the real growth occurs. Ask yourself, "Am I really ready to yield to God's will and let Him change me into what He wants me to be? Am I ready to be obedient?" Slowly and prayerfully read each insight which you have written. Come to God with one or more of these prayers as you consider each insight:

Lord, help me to . . .
Lord, I thank You so much for . . .
Lord, You are . . .
Lord, forgive me for . . .

As you do this, God will begin to change your character, and give you wisdom, growth, and new maturity. *"All scripture is inspired by God and profitable for teaching, for reproof, for correction, for training in righteousness."* (2 Timothy 3:16)

Other Helps:

- You do not have to complete all of these steps in one night. Relax and fully enjoy your Bible study! Remember that speed is not a goal.
- Study one chapter at a time.
- Watch out for this temptation: "I feel so good about my Christian growth, I don't think I need to study the Bible tonight."
- While you are studying, don't let yourself slip into the habit of, "Pete needs to hear this," or "This is just what my class needs to hear." Listen for yourself first, asking the Lord to change you, then you can share your insights with others.
- If you are having trouble finding time to memorize and meditate on Scripture during the week, incorporate Scripture memory into your Bible study time.
- Your morning QT is for fellowship with God, not for study, so praise God as you read and pray each morning and study and pray at night.

Will you make a commitment to have daily Bible study? If so, order two *Be Loyal* books now (See Resource Section, page 257). During Sessions 9 and 10, you will be starting independent Bible study in Matthew.

APPENDIX G
EVANGELISTIC
METHODOLOGY

"And according to Paul's custom, he went to them, and for three Sabbaths reasoned with them from the Scriptures, explaining and giving evidence that the Christ had to suffer and rise again from the dead, and saying, 'This Jesus whom I am proclaiming to you is the Christ.'" (Acts 17:2 & 3)

If a Christian is to be effective in sharing the Gospel, he must first be seeking to live a godly life. A believer who is living with the fruit of the Spirit is a tremendous endorsement for the power of the Gospel.

When possible, seek to develop relationships with people, then share Christ with them. This is called relationship evangelism. For example, there is a submarine sandwich restaurant near my home and I eat there frequently. I have made friends with the man and woman who work there and have developed a relationship. After building that relationship, I shared with them about Christ. I gave them a New Testament which included my testimony, an evangelistic booklet and a business card with a map to our church. They were very receptive. She said that the last time they were in church was 21 years ago when they were married. I wrote in her Bible, religion is based upon rules and regulations, but a relationship with Christ is based upon love. Building a relationship with a relative, bank teller, or hairstylist is another example of a possible evangelistic opportunity. *Developing an Evangelistic Strategy*, (Spiritual Application Project #5), is an example of relationship evangelism. During this

251

project, you develop a relationship with a friend or relative for several months before sharing the Gospel. Sometimes you cannot develop a relationship with a person before sharing, and must use initiative evangelism. Examples of this type of evangelism are, *Conducting An Evangelistic Survey*, (Spiritual Application Project #3), and *Giving An Evangelistic Booklet Away*, (Spiritual Application Project #2).

You should never feel that you have to rely strictly on initiative evangelism *or* relationship evangelism. When you are relying on the Holy Spirit for guidance, He will direct your approach. Don't fall into the trap of never witnessing to anyone because you haven't developed a "good enough" relationship.

When witnessing, we must never allow the fear of rejection to override the Lord's command to share the good news! We must totally embrace Jesus' teaching that when someone rejects the gospel, they are not rejecting you personally, they are actually rejecting God's forgiveness. The Bible says, *"The one who listens to you listens to Me, and the one who rejects you rejects Me, and he who rejects Me rejects the one who sent Me."* (Luke 10:16)

We must never let living a Godly life, as vitally important as that is, *substitute* for verbalizing the Gospel message. People need to hear *why* you are the way you are. Peter and John stated, "We cannot help speaking about what we have seen and heard." (Acts 4:20, NIV) They prayed, "Enable your servants to speak your Word with great boldness." (Acts 4:29, NIV) Imagine how effective Paul would have been in leading others to Christ if he would have said, "I'm just going to live a Godly life before people and when they ask me why I am the way I am, I will share the Gospel."

Jesus tells us to "Go and make disciples of all nations." (Matthew 28:19, NIV) In order for this command to be fulfilled, we must verbalize the Gospel.

APPENDIX H
EVANGELISTIC
APPROACHES
QUESTIONS & ANSWERS

1. This little booklet tells what it means to be a real Christian. Knowing Christ has been the best and most important decision of my life. He has given me peace, purpose, and happiness!

2. Through the years, have you come to know Jesus Christ in a personal way, or are you still on the way?

3. Have you met Jesus Christ yet, or do you feel that you are still looking for the truth?

4. Do you think about spiritual things often?

5. In all of time, who do you think has affected history the most? Why?

6. In your opinion, what is a Christian?

7. Do you know what the Bible says about eternal life?

8. Has anyone ever shared with you how to have a personal relationship with God?

9. (How to respond when someone says, "Jesus was a great teacher.") He said that He was the Son of God. If He lied, how can He be such a great teacher?

10. What do you think of Jesus Christ?

11. May I tell you how I know for sure that I am going to heaven?

12. Why should God receive you into His heaven?

13. a. Do you think heaven is a perfect place?

    b. How close have you come to living a perfect life?

    c. If God let you go to heaven as you are, what would happen to heaven's perfect record?

    d. Read 2 Corinthians 5:17 together, and explain the purpose of conversion.

14. a. If someone were to ask you to describe what a real Christian is, what would you tell them?

    b. Have you ever considered becoming a real Christian?

    c. Is there any good reason why you wouldn't want to invite Jesus Christ into your heart right now and ask Him to forgive your sin?

15. "_____, there are a few verses in the Bible that you might find interesting along these lines. Would you like to see them?"

16. I've heard you mention God's name several times. Do you know Him? Philippians 3:10

17. What is your opinion of …?
    (right, wrong, politics, a recent event, etc.?)

18. What do you think about your church experience now that you are away from home?

19. Do you take your religious beliefs more seriously or less seriously now that _____?

20. Isn't it amazing that Jesus actually said so many narrow things? Would you like to study His life to discover why He made such claims?

21. a. If you have five minutes, I can share what knowing Christ means to me.

    b. If he doesn't have time say, "I would like to encourage you to read this booklet before you go to bed tonight."

22. a. Have you come to the place in your spiritual life that you know for certain that if you died today you would go to heaven?

    b. Suppose you were to die today and you stood before God. If He asked "Why should I let you into my Heaven," what would you say?

OBJECTIONS WITH SCRIPTURAL ANSWERS

- I am too great a sinner. 1 Timothy 1:15

- I am inadequate. Philippians 4:13, 2 Corinthians 9:8

- There is too much to give up. Mark 8:36

- I will have to change my life. James 4:4

- I may be misunderstood. Proverbs 29:25

- It's too late. John 6:37

- I want to wait. Isaiah 55:6

- God is too good to banish anyone from heaven. Romans 2:4-5

- There is no God. Psalm 14:1

- Jesus Christ can't be the only way. John 14:6

APPENDIX I
RESOURCE
SECTION

As you or your church need additional "Operation Multiplication" materials, simply visit us online at www.ieaom.org, call (800) 880-1350, or FAX (800) 880-8465.

A CALL TO JOY, A CALL TO GROWTH, AND *SPIRITUAL JOURNALS*

A Call to Joy/A Call to Growth **Discipler's Pack**
A Call To Joy **Timothy's Pack**
A Call To Growth **Timothy's Pack**
Graduate Discipler's Pack
Discipler's Graduation Diplomas
A Call to Joy **Graduation Diplomas**
A Call to Growth **Graduation Diplomas**
Spiritual Journal (Hanks/Beacham)
My Spiritual Diary - for children 7–10 (Waters)
Four-Part Decision Forms
Implementor's Guide
Coordinator's Notebook
Operation Multplication **Workshop on CD** (Hanks)
Operation Multplication **Workshop on Cassette** (Hanks)
Steps to Peace with God
Steps to Peace with God in Spanish
Assured of Heaven **Cassette** (Hanks)
Assured of Heaven **CD** (Hanks)
The Great Commission **CD** (Hanks)

FEATURED BOOKS:

Born to Reproduce (Trotman)
Discipleship (Hanks/Shell)
If You Love Me (Hanks)
Everyday Evangelism (Hanks)
The Gift of Giving (Watts)
The Master Plan of Evangelism (Coleman)
Quiet Times in Luke (Hanks/Nelson)

Scripture Memory Packet
52 Scripture verses on color-coded cards covering six topics:
New Creations in Christ,
Trials and Temptations,
Abiding in Christ,
Holy Behavior,
Spreading the Good News, and
Discipleship.
Available in NIV, NASB, KJV, and NKJV and in the following colors:

Dark Blue	Slate Blue
Black	Burgundy
Teal	Dusty Rose

Victory Scripture Memory Books in NASB and KJV

ADDITIONAL NOTES

ADDITIONAL NOTES

ADDITIONAL NOTES

ADDITIONAL NOTES

ADDITIONAL NOTES

ADDITIONAL NOTES

NKJV
JOHN 1:12

But as many as received Him, to them He gave the right to become children of God, even to those that believe in His name.

JOHN 1:12

NKJV
WEEK 6

NKJV
1 JOHN 5:13

These things I have written to you who believe in the name of the Son of God, that you may know that you have eternal life, and that you may continue to believe in the name of the Son of God.

1 JOHN 5:13

NKJV
WEEK 10

NKJV
ROMANS 5:8

But God demonstrates His own love toward us, in that while we were still sinners, Christ died for us.

ROMANS 5:8

NKJV
WEEK 4

NKJV
PSALM 119:11

Your Word have I hidden in my heart, that I might not sin against You.

PSALM 119:11

NKJV
WEEK 8

NKJV
ROMANS 6:23

For the wages of sin is death, but the gift of God is eternal life in Christ Jesus our Lord.

ROMANS 6:23

NKJV
WEEK 2

---

5. From this moment forward, my life belongs to You and You alone.
6. I will love You, serve You, and tell others about You, and trust You to live Your life through me.
7. Thank you Lord, for coming into my life and for forgiving my sins today.

ROMANS 3:23
NKJV WEEK 1

For all have sinned and fall short of the glory of God.

ROMANS 3:23

The Sinner's Prayer
WEEK 7

1. Lord Jesus, I am a sinner,
2. But I am sorry for my sins.
3. I want to turn from my sins; I am willing to begin a new life with Your help.
4. Lord Jesus, please come into my heart and life right now.

(Turn card over)

HEBREWS 9:27
NKJV WEEK 3

It is appointed for men to die once, but after this the judgment.

HEBREWS 9:27

2 CORINTHIANS 5:17
NKJV WEEK 9

Therefore, if anyone is in Christ, he is a new creation; old things have passed away; behold, all things have become new.

2 CORINTHIANS 5:17

EPHESIANS 2:8 - 9
NKJV WEEK 5

For by grace you have been saved through faith, and that not of yourselves; it is the gift of God, not of works, lest anyone should boast.

EPHESIANS 2:8 - 9

JOHN 10:28
NKJV WEEK 11

And I give them eternal life, and they shall never perish, neither shall anyone snatch them out of My hand.

JOHN 10:28

ROMANS 3:23 — NIV — WEEK 1

For all have sinned and fall short of the glory of God.

ROMANS 3:23

HEBREWS 9:27 — NIV — WEEK 3

Man is destined to die once, and after that to face judgment.

HEBREWS 9:27

EPHESIANS 2:8 - 9 — NIV — WEEK 5

For it is by grace you have been saved, through faith — and this not from yourselves, it is the gift of God — not by works, so that no one can boast.

EPHESIANS 2:8 - 9

The Sinner's Prayer — WEEK 7

1. Lord Jesus, I am a sinner,
2. But I am sorry for my sins.
3. I want to turn from my sins; I am willing to begin a new life with Your help.
4. Lord Jesus, please come into my heart and life right now.

(Turn card over)

---

2 CORINTHIANS 5:17 — NIV — WEEK 9

Therefore, if anyone is in Christ, he is a new creation; the old has gone, the new has come!

2 CORINTHIANS 5:17

JOHN 10:28 — NIV — WEEK 11

I give them eternal life, and they shall never perish; no one can snatch them out of my hand.

JOHN 10:28

ROMANS 3:23 — NASB — WEEK 1

For all have sinned and fall short of the glory of God.

ROMANS 3:23

HEBREWS 9:27 — NASB — WEEK 3

It is appointed for men to die once and after this comes judgment.

HEBREWS 9:27

EPHESIANS 2:8 - 9 — NASB — WEEK 5

For by grace you have been saved through faith; and that not of yourselves, it is the gift of God; not as a result of works, that no one should boast.

EPHESIANS 2:8-9

ROMANS 6:23

For the wages of sin is death, but the gift of God is eternal life in Christ Jesus our Lord.

ROMANS 6:23

---

5. From this moment forward, my life belongs to You and You alone.
6. I will love You, serve You, and tell others about You, and trust You to live Your life through me.
7. Thank you Lord, for coming into my life and for forgiving my sins today.

ROMANS 6:23

For the wages of sin is death, but the free gift of God is eternal life in Christ Jesus our Lord.

ROMANS 6:23

ROMANS 5:8

But God demonstrates his own love for us in this: While we were still sinners, Christ died for us.

ROMANS 5:8

PSALM 119:11

I have hidden your word in my heart that I might not sin against you.

PSALM 119:11

ROMANS 5:8

But God demonstrates His own love toward us, in that while we were yet sinners, Christ died for us.

ROMANS 5:8

JOHN 1:12

Yet to all who received him, to those who believed in his name, he gave the right to become children of God.

JOHN 1:12

---

1 JOHN 5:13

I write these things to you who believe in the name of the Son of God so that you may know that you have eternal life.

1 JOHN 5:13

JOHN 1:12

But as many as received Him, to them He gave the right to become children of God, even to those who believe in His name.

JOHN 1:12

NASB
WEEK 8

PSALM 119:11

Thy word I have treasured in my heart, that I may not sin against Thee.

PSALM 119:11

5. From this moment forward, my life belongs to You and You alone.

6. I will love You, serve You, and tell others about You, and trust You to live Your life through me.

7. Thank you Lord, for coming into my life and for forgiving my sins today.

KJV
WEEK 2

ROMANS 6:23

For the wages of sin is death; but the gift of God is eternal life through Jesus Christ our Lord.

ROMANS 6:23

5. From this moment forward, my life belongs to You and You alone.

6. I will love You, serve You, and tell others about You, and trust You to live Your life through me.

7. Thank you Lord, for coming into my life and for forgiving my sins today.

NASB
WEEK 10

1 JOHN 5:13

These things I have written to you who believe in the name of the Son of God, in order that you may know that you have eternal life.

1 JOHN 5:13

KJV
WEEK 6

JOHN 1:12

But as many as received him, to them gave he power to become the sons of God, even to them that believe on his name.

JOHN 1:12

KJV
WEEK 8

PSALM 119:11

Thy word have I hid in mine heart, that I might not sin against Thee.

PSALM 119:11

1 JOHN 5:13

These things have I written unto you that believe on the name of the Son of God; that ye may know that ye have eternal life, and that ye may believe on the name of the Son of God.

1 JOHN 5:13

The Sinner's Prayer — WEEK 7

1. Lord Jesus, I am a sinner,
2. But I am sorry for my sins.
3. I want to turn from my sins; I am willing to begin a new life with Your help.
4. Lord Jesus, please come into my heart and life right now.

(Turn card over)

2 CORINTHIANS 5:17 — NASB — WEEK 9

Therefore if any man is in Christ, he is a new creature; the old things passed away; behold, new things have come.

2 CORINTHIANS 5:17

JOHN 10:28 — NASB — WEEK 11

I give eternal life to them, and they shall never perish; and no one shall snatch them out of My hand.

JOHN 10:28

ROMANS 3:23 — KJV — WEEK 1

For all have sinned, and come short of the glory of God.

ROMANS 3:23

HEBREWS 9:27 — KJV — WEEK 3

It is appointed unto men once to die, but after this the judgment.

HEBREWS 9:27

EPHESIANS 2:8 - 9 — KJV — WEEK 5

For by grace are ye saved through faith; and that not of yourselves: it is the gift of God: Not of works, lest any man should boast.

EPHESIANS 2:8 - 9

The Sinner's Prayer — WEEK 7

1. Lord Jesus, I am a sinner,
2. But I am sorry for my sins.
3. I want to turn from my sins; I am willing to begin a new life with Your help.
4. Lord Jesus, please come into my heart and life right now.

(Turn card over)

2 CORINTHIANS 5:17 — KJV — WEEK 9

Therefore if any man be in Christ, he is a new creature: old things are passed away; behold, all things are become new.

2 CORINTHIANS 5:17

JOHN 10:28 — KJV — WEEK 11

And I give unto them eternal life; and they shall never perish, neither shall any man pluck them out of my hand.

JOHN 10:28

We are pleased that you chose to study *A Call To Growth*, and have now completed this intermediate level of discipleship training.

If this experience has been particularly meaningful to you, we hope you will take the time to complete and mail the card below. Your evaluation would be appreciated. May God bless your continued growth and ministry of spiritual multiplication! Thank You.

Please complete and mail.

A CALL TO GROWTH II

I was a Discipler ☐ Timothy ☐ Name: _____

Address: _____ City: _____ ST: _____ Zip: _____

- Which section helped you grow the most: _____

- God has worked in my life in the area(s) of: _____

- I am now personally committed to: _____

- I believe this course could be strengthened by: _____

BUSINESS REPLY MAIL

FIRST-CLASS MAIL   PERMIT NO. 57   SALADO, TX

POSTAGE WILL BE PAID BY THE ADDRESSEE

INTERNATIONAL EVANGELISM
PO BOX 1174
SALADO   TX   76571-9979